Praise for Sarah Ann May
and *There Is Always Hope*

"This is really encouraging! I have been through some very bumpy times in my marriage and it is so hard to consider it joy. Thank you for the hope that it is worth it."—**Melissa Haag**

"Your words though are solid truth! What an amazing God we serve."—**Natalie Butsch**

"Oh, what a beautiful reminder that we are all weak and in need of a Savior—one who offers us hope for our broken hearts and broken pieces. Thank you for sharing. May God continue to give you hope for your journey."—**Blest but Stress**

"Beautiful! I loved this line in particular: *Now, I know that comfort was false, it was nothing but hiding.* Isn't that just a powerful truth right there? Comfort feels so true and wise . . . but so often it is smoke and mirrors and anything but safe!"—**Karrilee Aggett**

"Such a beautiful post, straight from your heart to mine that blessed me and encouraged me to reach out to you and thank you for the wonderful HOPE . . . which have blessed and encouraged me daily. You are one awesome woman of God. May he be powerfully with you in the years to come as he continues to grow in your learning upon His everlasting arms."—**Mary Gems**

THERE IS ALWAYS
HOPE

SARAH ANN MAY

ARGYLE FOX
PUBLISHING

For Zach

Our life together now is worth
every moment of the past.
Thank you for clinging
to Hope alongside me.

Mark 10:9

Contents

A Note from the Author

Why didn't anyone ever tell me that? Shouldn't someone have let me know? Why didn't I know that already? I wish I had known!

These are questions and statements I have uttered to myself or lamented aloud frequently. Daily, almost. But then, I wonder, did someone tell me and I just didn't listen? Did someone tell me, but I forgot? Or truly, was it a piece of information that somehow, during my life, I had just never acquired until the moment it was learned, occasionally in the hardest way?

We are often required to encourage another or give advice to another about an issue we have no experience with. While I have a great love for those who have given me wisdom in the midst of tumultuous experiences as well as the times I could do it for another, the best conversations, the exchanges that stick out to me the most, are the ones where my heart has needed the same words I am sharing with another. C.S. Lewis says, "Friendship is born at the moment when one man says to another 'What!? You too? I thought no one but myself.'"[1]

We need each other's words, we need each other's

experiences, we need each other's successes and failings.

In the writing world, one of the most discussed topics is having an ideal reader. The writer needs to know who those words swirling around in their heads are for in order to best get across the information necessary for that specific person in time. However, one point that is sure to be made by the experts is that one should not make oneself the ideal reader.

Confession: I have never been much good at this, which is probably why I am far from a famous writer. For my personal desires and purposes, I need to be intimately connected to the topic. I need to have whatever I am saying be something I feel or have felt deeply. The words written for public view have to be something that I also need to hear. Words, perhaps, that fall under the realm of *Why didn't anyone tell me?*

Honestly, though, after some consideration, it's actually not even my current self who would usually fit the bill as my ideal reader. Instead, it is more often the person I was in the past. The person who did not yet know the things no one had told her.

For example, what would I say to the five-year-old girl so very afraid of the dark; to the twelve-year-old who had no clue how to deal with a friend all of a sudden not wanting to be her friend anymore; to the sixteen-year-old who was trying to balance high school and boys and driving a car without getting lost (both literally and figuratively); to the nineteen-year-old who had her heart broken; to the twenty-two-year-old newly-wed with a new job in a new state; to the twenty-five-year-old with a baby completely dependent upon her; to the thirty-one-year-old who hit a road bump in marriage so hard it could have totaled the whole thing?

We often say if we could just go back and tell our past self this, this, and this, everything would have turned out differently. But would it? *Back to the Future* is probably not the most intellectual example to throw in here, but in my recollection of the tales of Marty and Doc, going back and making changes, any changes, did not seem to help the future out; in fact, it damaged it.

As lovely as we think it would be, changing our past is not going to bring sudden happiness and perfection. While I don't completely agree with Rafiki when he whacks Simba on the head and tells him it doesn't matter, it's in the past, I highly agree with his next statement, "You can't change it, but you can learn from it."[2]

Mother Teresa said, "Beautiful are the ways of God if we allow him to use us as he wants."[3] When life experience is our teacher, we have the opportunity to store away those hard-fought lessons for a reason far greater than our own life's peace. With our life, we have the opportunity to change another's.

You see, not everyone has hit the milestones you have, not everyone has gone through the same suffering that you have, and not everyone who has similar sufferings and experiences has made it to the other side of them. Kristen Welch, author and founder of Mercy House, encourages us to "let what God has done for you affect everything you do for others."[4] There will always be someone further ahead of you and there will always be someone coming up behind. One of my jobs as a believer is to accept those hands that are there to pull me up, but to also reach back with my own hands and pull up another.

We cannot do anything about what is done because, as they say, it is done. But we can do something about how we use what has happened in our lives not only for ourselves, but the ones around us. By living in community, sharing our stories, and saying out loud the things we know we need to hear, instead of pretending as if we have it all together, the ones we walk alongside will see, will hear, will have the opportunity to learn without it having to always come to them through the hardest ways. Like Hamilton told Eliza, "If it takes fighting a war for us to meet, it will have been worth it."[5]

Though comparing life's challenges to war might seem like a gross exaggeration, when we think about it as it says in Scripture about flesh fighting against spirit, it can be seen that the difficulties we face are more warlike after all. Because of that, I want to make known some of my hardest learned lessons, the things I would love to tell my younger self, but can't. Instead, I share them with you, in hopes that by hearing them you do not have to say, "I wish someone would have told me." Rather, you can say, "I'm so glad I already knew."

Here are a few lessons I've learned along the way and am glad to share with you.

• It's natural to be afraid of the dark. Fear doesn't make you weak. It most likely means you have an overactive imagination, which just happens to be an amazing character quality that births creativity.

• Friendships are hard, but they are worth fighting for. If there is someone you want to remain in your life, take the time to let them know that.

• Friendships are hard, and sometimes they need to be let go. It's okay for it to hurt even as it's also a relief.

• Friendships are hard, and sometimes friendships just end. Even if neither of you knows why nor really wanted it to happen, it just happens.

• Some boys are insane, emotional, and careless with your heart. Some boys are kind, thoughtful, and careful with your heart. That second group of boys will still do stupid stuff.

• It's good to forgive anyone for anything. It doesn't mean you'll still be in each other's lives. The forgiveness is more for your heart anyway.

• Being an introvert is a dang good character quality, so never apologize for it. It just means you were created to serve this world in a different way with a different view.

• It is always a good idea to have the conversation. Even if you are nervous, even if you are terrified, even if you will cry the whole time you are talking. It is still better than leaving needed words unsaid.

• Almost everything is hard the first time you do it, that's why you need to do it a second time and a third and keep going until it is easier. Except if what you are doing is illegal, just stop that now!

• If something comes easy to you that does not come easy to others it doesn't mean it's not a valuable skill, it means you found one of your gifts. Be thankful.

• You do not have to prove anything to anyone. Be confident that you can feel what is best for you. If you do not want to do something, don't do it. If you want to do something, keep at it. Friends will encourage you in either case, non-friends will pressure you on just one. Stick with the encouragers.

• If a boy breaks up with you because you get scared by scary movies then he is an idiot and you are better off without him.

• If you feel a calling deep inside, asking you to do something you have never done, it does not make you feel better to ignore it. Step out in faith knowing the One who has called you to it is trying to do something beautiful for someone, somewhere, and He WILL make you capable.

• Lifting weights is fun and makes you feel like a superhero and even though you know it is totally cliché, throwing them down in dramatic fashion every once in a while makes you feel rough and tough in the best possible way.

• Parenting is all kinds of hard and all kinds of beautiful and all kinds of exhausting and all kinds of sanctifying and pretty much the best thing I have ever been allowed to do.

• If you're feeling like a hot mess, say you're feeling like a hot mess. If you're having a crappy day, say you're having a crappy day. If you are in love with where you are in life, just say so! Your honesty is sure to help another be honest as well!

• If one day it feels as if life is falling apart, well, it might just be, but that doesn't mean it won't get built back up again, usually in a different and better way.

• Pivots in life do not mean you chose wrong the first time, it means that part is done and it's time to move on to the next.

• And lastly, as you dive into this book, here is the biggest lesson of all: No matter what, no matter where you find your-self at this very moment or where you are still stuck in the past, no matter the difficulty that might be taking over every ounce of your being, THERE IS ALWAYS HOPE!

Praying for you as you go forward, both in these words ahead and in life itself,

Sarah Ann May

THERE IS ALWAYS
HOPE

1

The Bomb

I remember what his face looked like. The expression of complete regret and fear will be burned into my memory forever, along with the eyes that gazed back with a glimpse of relief because of what was about to be unloaded from the mind behind them. He sat on the couch opposite mine, knees apart serving as a place to set his elbows with hands up ready to catch his head if it fell forward from the raw emotion swimming inside. I knew what was coming, all the while wishing my all too spot-on womanly intuition was having an uncommon failure. Even though it was the last thing I wanted to hear, I begged for him to just say it, say it out loud, because then the ice would be broken, then it would be out in the light, then we could move forward . . .

All of the road, begun from birth, is a series of hard and lovely. What is it that Frederick Buechner said? "Here is the world. Beautiful and terrible things will happen. Don't be afraid."[6] The first two statements are so easily said while the last command, at times, so heartbreakingly difficult. How is it possible to not be afraid when you find yourself in a moment where your greatest fear, the described "terrible," has become a reality?

I know little about the medical field, but I do know that the moment the line on the screen showing life changes from peaks and valleys to a flat plane is one of the worst that can happen. When it does occur, buzzers sound, warning bells ring, and many highly trained individuals converge in a necessary flurry to use all the skills in which they were so carefully trained in order to restore the normalcy of the peaked and valleyed rhythm. Peaks and valleys prove that there is life. They prove that the heart is still a part of this world.

Typical low points, the standard inevitable frustrations we face, may have you singing "the sun'll come out tomorrow" if you are one of the plucky ones, or doing your best Scarlett impression and "thinking about it tomorrow" for the more dramatic souls. Tomorrow is, in fact, another day, and the desire to continually place things on its agenda to free our emotions from dealing with the issue today is a temptation for sure. Some valleys, however, go well beyond standard and when they come, feel as if they are blowing your life apart instead of simply reminding you that you are still alive. These bombs in life make the valley resemble a landscape more in common with a giant crater.

There are too many real-life situations to take this matter lightly. Each of our minds can conjure up memories of news footage where both the innocent and the guilty have had their lives destroyed by a literal bomb. These explosions send hearts, minds, and bodies reeling in mere seconds and yet leave an aftermath that requires those seconds, times a million, to fully pick up the pieces, process through them, rebuild, and move on.

It is nearly impossible to roam alive on this earth and not come across news of such terrible tragedies. There are handfuls of countries at this very moment whose people live this life of dodging on a daily basis. These are places where steps are trodden delicately, corners are checked before turning, and eyes are cut side to side looking for warning signs of danger. Former chairman of the Joint Chiefs of Staff General Martin Dempsey even declared in 2012, "[W]e are living in the most dangerous time in my lifetime, right now," only to have to recant a year later to say, "No, this is the most dangerous the world has **ever** been."[7] God in heaven, protect us all, please.

Even still, the majority of us, though we witness events through media and are called upon to help with our resources, will never experience the fear and danger that come from a physical bomb. But, for each of us, there will be or has been a time when other not-so-tangible bombs go off in life. They may not bring the physical destruction that one crafted with wire, metal, and plastic can, but these crisis situations that blow up our individual worlds can leave a similar aftermath, both emotionally and spiritually, of distress, confusion, and upheaval that takes us as long or even longer from which to recover.

Author Catherine Marshall experienced a good deal of trauma in her life with the death of her first husband, chronic health issues, and the typical pitfalls of a person who has risen in fame. Her book *A Closer Walk* shares insights taken from her personal journals in which she recorded, "How is it, I marveled, that bad news has a way of invading human life so suddenly? Trouble rings no warning bells. Adversity and sorrow walk in to life on rubber soles."[8]

They can come with little warning. At least in the movies you are privy to the soundtrack faintly present in the background, guiding your emotions and your intuitions as the melodies and minor chords elevate your blood pressure to clue you in that a dramatic scene about to take place. Life does not have a soundtrack, but it does have something else. The world calls it *intuition* or *conscience*. In Christian circles we understand that feeling in your heart or gut that seems to be warning you of danger or reminding you of what is right as the guidance of the Holy Spirit. When Jesus left earth to sit at the right hand of the Father, He promised us a helper. The Holy Spirit is that helper. The Holy Spirit's job is to guide, to intercede, to be Jesus with us always, reminding us of who we are because we are in Christ; and so, when we feel that little nudge (or big push depending on the moment) in our heart and soul, we must learn to pay attention, to listen, because that is our holy helper letting us know that something is coming that requires us to remember all He has taught before. But, even then we do not always listen well.

Maybe, perhaps, trouble did ring warning bells and the Spirit within enabled you to hear a faint ticking noise in the depths of your being and you brushed it off, never imagining it was a cautionary sound to a coming dramatic blow. Maybe, perhaps, that monotonous tick, tick, tick might have become even louder yet, but piling things upon the place the noise appeared to be coming from while earnestly expecting it to just stop on its own seemed to be the best course of action.

Again, there is also a chance that you were caught completely unaware. No pretending or avoiding, you found yourself at the complete mercy of a surprise attack, a moment where life blew up without so much as a sign of its appearance and then leaving you in its aftermath with shock, fear, devastation, questions, and little energy to process it all.

Not all bombs deploy. Some are found ahead of time,

whether by chance or by following the telltale ticking, and diffused before they can do their greatest harm. Sure, there are consequences from just the knowledge that the potential for an explosion existed, but without everything being torn apart it seems much easier to move along with life afterwards. But whether it snuck in on those rubber soles, faintly warned you of its imminent arrival, or marched in with a twisted version of "Pomp and Circumstance," we will all find ourselves on the spectrum of little "t" trauma to Grey's Anatomy-level drama at some time in our life.

So, my question to you now is not if you have experienced this, but which you have experienced? Is there a bomb that has just gone off in life that has caused your heart to distrust others and to desire instead to hide from them all? Or are you fully present and desperate to heal, but can't quite find the way? Maybe it isn't you, but you are watching someone you love experience the aftermath instead. Maybe you are seeking a way to help another who has already sent themselves into hiding in plain sight, their heart desperate to forget? Or maybe they are ready and willing to seek the way to recovery, but are stuck without guidance of how to get there.

Take a moment here, friend. Breathe. Think. Let those thoughts so crowded in your mind that none seem clear begin to move to the center stage and come into focus. Zone in. Can you pinpoint it? Can you search back in your history to see that moment that sent you reeling? Perhaps it is still living so close to the forefront of your mind that it is impossible to look anywhere without seeing it. It is the giant elephant taking up all the space in the room. But know this: you are not the only one with an elephant to contend with.

Our hearts know that life is not easy. Cliché or not, truism or not, those words are apt to flutter out of mouths both in compassion and sarcasm at each and every scenario, from sitting with a friend crying over the loss of a job to standing over your child who is in the depths of despair because you refuse to hand him the shoe lying two inches from his fingertips that he swears he cannot reach on his own. (Not that this happens in the middle of my kitchen floor by one of three boys on an almost daily basis.)

However, we convince ourselves that for some people that statement is not true, that for some, life is a continuous ease of success and happiness. Even David, future king of Israel, fell prey to this idea as he poured out his anguish in Psalm 10 asking God why He was so far away from him all the while assuming his enemies' ways were always secure as they moved from generation to generation without calamity.

If required to pinpoint my greatest desire for the life of another, apart from them knowing Christ in their life, it would be that they not believe the deceit that says others have it easy. Even if you look around and see that one person, you know who they are, who appears to have it all, don't be fooled. Like the too-good-to-be-true beautiful pools of water in the desert, it's a mirage created within your head. If a real conversation was begun, instead of the imaginary one you assume will transpire, that picture-perfect person would be able to give you, quite quickly I'd bet, a list of struggles they face, the ways they feel insecure, and their need for something more in their life to make it all okay.

By this time, you may be wondering why a book promising that there is always hope seems to be taking such a discouraging turn. Admittedly, I may have even bummed myself out a bit, but for good reason, because, friend, in all honesty, the best thing that can happen to you is for life to NOT be easy. If it were, there would be no need of help with anything, ever. At first glance this may sound like a life worth living. One of utopia, kumbayas, and always clean houses. Is it even possible to imagine a day with no arguing, no hatred, no mistakes, no missteps, no misunderstandings, or no misspoken words? All steps would be positive, but then all steps might be taken alone because if you know all and can accomplish all, what need is there for another, for a helper, a confidant, a partner in (metaphorical) crime?

Take those most valuable lessons you have learned and consider the people you have met and where you are now because of the difficulties you faced in this not-so-easy life. Let the memories be revisited of friends who have walked alongside you in dark times, the backs that have carried each other's burdens, the forged friendships built on solid foundations growing exponentially because of what you went through together. They all came at the cost of losing something. These not-easy moments, these growths from depths traversed, came as a direct result of having to lose not-so-positive relationships, to lose false peace that came through putting trust in the wrong things, to lose the shield of self-sufficiency and self-survival in order to lean on another.

Asking for a hand up is one of the most humbling experiences, but the damage that comes from pretending all is well keeps us from the life-giving relationships. What would be the point of those long coffee shop conversations with a kindred spirit about life's journey if everything was all good?

More importantly, if life were easy and we could go zooming along with no problems, what would be the point of praising our Creator? What would be the need of leaning on our

23

Savior? What would be the point of having His Spirit within us guiding and directing our steps?

Blubbered forth from these lips have been abundant prayers that the words on these pages reach not only hearts that already know that they do indeed have a Savior, but also those of you who do not yet have that personal relationship with Jesus.

Oh, to you who has a heart that already understands deep down that you are known and loved and will be reminded again and again through this book that you are KNOWN and LOVED, you have in your possession the greatest gift ever given. But please, present among us, let there be sweet spirits who are confused when they are told that they were created for a purpose. Let there be ones who think they have it all together or naively assume they have felt the hardest things they will feel and have not yet experienced a bomb in life that blew everything they thought they knew to the four winds. This wish does not come from a desire to provoke another so that they can face reality sooner or be told in a gloating air of wisdom that "you ain't seen nothing yet." No, this wish stems from the desire that when you find yourself in a moment where the ticking stops and nothing is like it was before, you are prepared with soul-filling words that will make it just a little bit easier to walk through the after and beyond.

We were created to glorify God and enjoy Him forever. 1 Corinthians 10:31 tells us that "whether you eat or drink or whatever you do, do it all for the glory of God." (NIV) "Whatever we do" means EVERYTHING we do, and it is done for His glory. Many, many times that glory comes through the hard and difficult.

When we understand that there will be bad, we are better prepared to see the good, even when we do not understand why, at the time, the bad happens.

The wise writer of Proverbs 3:5 encourages us to "trust in the Lord with all your heart and lean not on your own understanding" (ESV) for a reason. The reason is simply that things will happen in our lives that we cannot comprehend. You cannot lean on your understanding when you do not understand. That would be a trust fall into empty arms. The bombs that go off in your life leave you in a state of confusion, of not understanding. Whether it is the why, the how, or the what, you are left with no personal wisdom on which to lean. Our minds and bodies must have something to rest on, something to prop up against, and if it is ourselves we are counting on, we will eventually find ourselves face down in the rubble. Here is where we begin to see our need for hope, and my goal is to show you how it is always there.

No one walks through life unscathed. The caliber changes, the damage ranges from minimal to extensive, but for each of us, tough times present themselves nonetheless. There are seasons when the word *impossible* seems like the only word weighty enough to fully explain what has instigated the weary soul within you. There are seasons for us all when we just want to pause life, come up to the surface and breathe.

It takes one to know one. And as Paul says in Philippians 1:12, "I want you to know, brothers, that what has happened to me has really served to advance the gospel." (ESV)

As I sit, it has been seven-plus years since the pretty picture I had built in my mind of life and family was blown to bits. My husband, the one whom my soul loves, sat on the couch opposite me and confessed that a friendship with another woman, a woman I was very close to, had grown into, not just an inappropriate friendship for a married man, but an affair. I felt in an instant my world stop and then shift off its well-turning axis. Thought after thought passed before me, like a mystery drama where at the end they replay every scene, only this time showing the ways the brilliant detective picked up the clues that enabled him to solve the crime.

I was that detective, suddenly overwhelmed with all the clues and all the tick, tick, ticks I had heard and yet blocked out, covered up, or was afraid to believe. This trauma was both all of a sudden and dripping with warnings. It was everything, but in the end it did not leave me with nothing. It left me with a heart-changing phoenix that would emerge from all that ash.

Part of me wants to stop here and defend my husband by sharing the idols in his life he was feeding, the briefness of that relationship, what God has done in his heart since, and a million other parts of our story, but I won't. That is not the point.

Another part wants to proclaim that God designed marriage to be beautiful and to honor Him and that He can redeem, if He chooses, any marriage no matter the circumstances, but that is not the point either.

The point is, that within just the few moments it took to utter a sentence, my world was rocked and nothing would ever be how it was again.

The point is, while this one bomb in my life was sparked by marital issues, there have been others as well. There are countless situations and circumstances that set off a fuse in the lives of us all. I have been a witness to a grand array; we all have.

The point is, I have learned more about myself through the dark times as I was searching for the light than during any other time in life. Why? Because of hope.

On this earth full of joys and failures, experiences of elation and devastation, we convince ourselves, more than once, that these individual moments are what define us, are most important, are the reason we live, or are what we are forced to live with. In these moments, no matter how serious or frivolous they may seem to our eyes or the eyes of another, there is hope.

There is always hope.

In that same Psalm in which David lamented the enemy he was facing, he was also rejoicing in the God whose presence he had questioned just verses before. Psalm 10 ends with David's remembering and singing out loud, "You, Lord, hear the desire of the afflicted; you encourage them, and you listen to their cry." (NIV) David, even amid the frustrations of the assumed silence, had hope that His God heard his cry.

No two people will have the same story, even in the most similar of circumstances. We are exquisite individuals created for unique purposes and thus the lives we live must be unique as well. You see, we are each our own thoughtfully planned creation, which means in life we will face our own set of circumstances. However, we are also each part of a community larger than just ourselves and our own special uniqueness is placed within bigger communities not just for our own purpose but for those around us as well. So, while God's design touches each of us specifically, it is also for all of us together, and it is my firm belief that we are all learning the same core lessons; those lessons just come in a million different ways.

Scripture defines this community as the body of Christ. Romans 12:4-5 says that "For as in one body we have many members, and the members do not all have the same function, so we, though many, are one body in Christ and individually members one of another." (ESV) If you are a believer, one of the communities you are in is this body, the body of Christ, also known as the Church. Not just a building in which you may or may not attend on a regular basis, but a bigger-than-you-can-imagine group of people who share this core belief in Jesus, who work together as a whole by each doing their own individual part.

It is because of this body in which we are individual members but together as one, that it's possible for our Sovereign Father to speak directly to the heart of each individually designed life using the exact same truths through the words He left us with, His Word. Within the bombs we each face, along the spectrum of small trauma to life-stopping drama, we can look there to find the same truths that will help us up and lead us on. And it's all done for His Glory and our good so that we may see Him, so that we may see hope.

I am just one little person and this is just one little story. The trip to understanding hope, seeing hope, and clinging to hope is not without its difficulties, but the view on the other side is incomparably worth the time it takes to get there.

The words you read throughout the pages of this book are not written by a being you would be tempted to compare yourself to on the street, in the store, or maybe even sitting next to you on the couch, which could possibly make you feel you are lacking in some way, damaged, different, or not enough. These words come from a fellow sinner, a fellow hurting heart, a fellow life-bomb survivor, who understands that on my own I have nothing, but with Christ I have everything I need.

Like Brennan Manning, I'm just a beggar telling another beggar where to find a piece of bread.

That is where we go from here.

2

Biblical Hope

*The text message came out of the blue, but then again, maybe not.
When you believe your life is in the hands of your Heavenly Father,
nothing happens by accident, and receiving a text full of life-changing,
paradigm-shifting words had to have been very much on purpose. In
the corner of the kitchen, surrounded by the noise of three rambunc-
tious boys in the adjacent playroom, I read this on the tiny screen in
front of me . . .*

Rejoice in the Lord alone.

Hope in the Lord alone.

Rest in the Lord alone.

Be satisfied in the Lord alone.

*Was I supposed to be doing this now, was I supposed to already
have been doing this, was I supposed to forget about dealing with my
husband and just focus on the Lord? Did the sender think I was
lacking in some way and was trying to give me advice on how to make
it better? Thoughts swirled around with raw emotion until it all settled
with the answer: Yes.*

*Yes, I needed to be doing this. Yes, I needed to already be doing
this. Yes, I needed to focus on the Lord and not worry about dealing so*

much with my husband. Previous thoughts matter not, what matters is that this wise counsel would make it better. It was advice that would narrow the focus of my attention. Life, thoughts, emotions, actions, everything in the aftermath of this bomb had become chaotic, but now I was given the bullseye. The center circle, the place your aim is shooting for, is in the Lord . . . alone.

Much like the perfect Christmas gift that's unexciting to open, but then proves itself irreplaceable days later, these words first brought a little confusion and a little bit of defensiveness, but quickly became an invaluable resource on which to look back. One text message, four sentences, and a spiritual awakening that might never be topped in my lifetime, but then again, who am I to put God in that kind of box?

C ore strength is essential for any structure, including the one that carries you around everywhere you go. We all need a solid center, a firm foundation that can withstand forces that, whether independently or as a byproduct of other things, have the potential to knock down whatever they come in contact with.

Have you ever watched a tree during a hurricane? Growing up in the Southeast but away from the coast gave me plenty of experience with hurricanes, while also thankfully keeping us away from the initial brunt of the storm. At age fourteen, I remember standing on my front porch watching as the winds of Opal pushed trees farther past their breaking point than I ever imagined them being able to go, only to see them straighten right back up with the next gust.

Just recently in 2017 as Hurricane Irma made her presence known in Georgia, I watched with my boys as the seventy-five-year-old pecan trees in our yard stood tall despite torrential rain and category-four winds coming at them only to, after the storm dissipated, ride our bikes around the neighborhood to find huge oaks of a similar age toppled over on almost every corner. The difference? Looking into the trunks that were now exposed to the eye revealed a hollow core. There was nothing solid, no strong center on the inside to keep those trees firmly planted. No matter the regal beauty they held on the outside, being empty on the inside left them subject to destruction.

Life without hope leaves us hollow. Without a hope to hold on to we are left desperately trying to fill a void with items and people of our own making, shoving them inside us one after the other to see if the next one will work when all the previous ones failed. Kate Winslet's whimsical British voice from the film *The Holiday* cannot help but appear in my thoughts in regards to this scenario. "We are a square peg and a round hole," she says as she tries to again understand her complicated and damaging relationship with Jasper. But then moments later, similar words come out, but this time with a different tone entirely. Instead of the sad confusion of the earlier statement she now proceeds with a exasperated and enlightened tone, "Yes! Very square peg! Very round hole!"

Somewhere between her first statement and her second a lightbulb went off and clarity reigned. That is the moment where hope moves in and fills the void. That is the moment where finally, a different word and a different perspective help make every little piece come together to create a big picture that has up until now been out of view. Regardless of the catalyst in each specific case, in this moment an understanding happens that in an instant changes the trajectory of your life.

Hope does not happen by chance. You are not a lottery

number waiting to be called so that millions of hopes can flood into your life. Hope, like the text message I received, is very much on purpose and is present in the moment you need it, the moment we all need it, always. But what exactly is hope? Well, first, let's think about what it is not.

It's easy to mix up words, their meanings and their pronunciations. I live a daily life of a word being on the tip of my tongue as my brain struggles to formulate the sounds that it cannot seem to remember. It takes a little wind out of your sails when you are trying to get an important point across only to have to stop and insert the phrase, "What's that word that starts with an *s* and means such and such? Well, that's the word I'm thinking of right now that would bring so much clarity to my point." It's only second in frustration to my "Somewhere in the Bible it says something kind of like this" points. Search engines were created for people like me. Thank you to Google for your help and thank you, friends, for just going with it and understanding me anyway, or at least pretending to.

It can actually be pretty cute when you screw up words. If you are a mama, you know there are a few words that your kids say the wrong way, and inside you would kind of love for them to never figure out, or at least not any time soon. Then if you hear someone try to correct them that angry-faced, teeth-gritting, wide-eyed, silent stare gets blasted in their direction, because what right do they have to correct my baby, thus de-cute-ifying some of their vocabulary? My oldest son for years called instructions, *con*structions. Every time he opened a new LEGO set and had to get the *constructions* out I thought my heart would burst from the adorableness of it all. I have seriously spent hours just sitting next to him during the LE-GO-building process, not to help mind you, but just to hear him utter the phrase, "Okay, what do the constructions say to do next?"

Unfortunately, not all mistakes are as cute as kiddos saying *pasketti* or *consolidated onions* or those hilarious but also embarrassing moments, when the *tr* in truck got replaced with an *f*. God bless it when you're at a parade and a fire truck drives by.

I bet the autocorrect feature on cell phones alone has caused many a dramatic situation as words and information get crossed and feelings get hurt. Do not even get me started on the inability to read someone's tone in a written message. I have sent MANY a self-corrected, clarification text or email just to make sure that what was said was taken in the way it was meant to be taken so that drama does not ensue! Later we will talk about listing fears and you can be assured that fear of being misunderstood is high on my list!

Now, let's move on to those words with multiple meanings. I am not referring to homonyms such as "My son hit a bat with a bat," which he did not do, but totally would, but to words that might have carried one meaning in the past, and then over time, through generations or in different cultures, have come to mean incredibly different things.

One morning in a nearby coffee shop, I ran into a friend and old neighbor. We spent a few minutes catching up on what had been going on in our lives and with our children and as he told me about how "wide open" life was for them it took a bit of time for my mind to change the meaning of that phrase from being "pretty vacant and available" to what he meant which was "full-throttle." Definitions are important, both for understanding another and being understood yourself.

Proverbs 18:21 says, "death and life are in the power of the tongue." (ESV) If our words do not carry life to another, they

33

have no choice but to carry with them a bit of death instead. At times, just the simple misunderstanding of a definition can change that life-giving statement to one of the opposite kinds because instead of it hitting the heart with truth, it comes with a different message.

There are words that God created and are written in His Word that the world over time has changed slightly and understood a little differently, thus dangerously changing, for our minds at least, what truth is. For example, take the word *joy*. In the world, we think of joy as meaning happiness that comes from success or good fortune or just something you like happening. You enjoy that, whatever that is, so therefore you must have joy. In reality, what God intended was for us to know that joy can always be present. When Philippians 4:4 tells us to "Rejoice in the Lord always, I will say it again: Rejoice!" (ESV) It is because there is something to rejoice about and there is always a cause for joy. Joy can be found in the deepest sorrows, because joy does not depend on the situations that you find yourself in. "You will fill me with joy in your presence," says Psalm 16:11 (NIV), and then Peter tells us in 1 Peter 1 that we will be "filled with an inexpressible and glorious joy." (NIV) Joy comes from being in Christ.

Hope is another of those words that has seen its meaning change over time.

Hope, through the view of the world, can seem so much like a wish. Like a desire for something that might never be, might never come to fruition, and then all that is left is a longing that will not be filled or a yearning now pressed down deep in an attempt to have it be forgotten. This definition is not only incorrect but has disastrous consequences when held.

A *New York Post* article about a woman who committed suicide included the note she had posted on social media to say, "See you later." Within it she writes, "I have accepted that hope is nothing more than delayed disappointment, and I am just plain old-fashioned tired of feeling tired."[9]

The words of this young woman simultaneously broke my heart and refueled my desire to not just share hope but to make sure others knew exactly what it was. No, you darling girl, that is not hope, and I am so very sorry that is the only hope you ever knew. But oh, how many understand it the same way, and oh, how many of us who do know about true hope don't live like we do?

As a test, I began to pay attention to how often I used the word *hope* and in what ways I was using it. For example, a text to a friend might read "I hope you had a good week," or thinking in my head, "I really hope Zach gets home on time tonight," or "I hope Auburn wins," which is said many times around our house in the fall! When I use the word *hope* in these ways, I am essentially saying it would be nice if this specific thing happened. I am throwing a request in the air and wishing for it to come true for my own benefit and sometimes for the benefit of others, but rarely is it ever for the benefit of my spirit. In those times I am not only misusing the word *hope*, but I am giving a false interpretation of it to others.

This word, as with many others, is used flippantly and, personally, I would love to make it a focus to change the way I use the word *hope*, not because I think people who use hope in its varied definitions are terrible people who obviously hate Jesus, but because I want to train my heart and mind to focus instead on the true hope, so that when that word comes from my lips it carries weight with it. When we live our lives with the incorrect understanding of hope, when we assume it is nothing more than delayed disappointment, then we are hoping for things that might never come true, that might never be. In these cases our hope is not real, it is not set upon a truth that never fails.

You see, in truth, real hope, biblical hope, hope in all its created meaning, is unfailing.

At the age of four I became a Christian, or so I'm told. Occasionally, deep in the recesses of my brain, I can conjure up some random memories from that early time in my life which include, but are not limited to, having to climb over a gate in someone's back yard to walk to the high school football stadium on a Friday night, where I sat on concrete bleachers and got to eat a Tootsie Roll Pop as a treat. I think I spent more time looking for the Native American on the wrapper shooting his bow and arrow at the stars than I ever did paying attention to the actual game. Unfortunately, that milestone moment during which my heart opened itself up to the only One who can save has never been one I remember. However, having been told the story many times, this is what I know.

While my older brother was talking about having asked Jesus into his heart, John D., our sweet and sassy little pastor, was asking my brother questions about what he thought, what he said, what he thinks would happen now, and so on. Apparently, my little blonde and also sweet and sassy self was listening intently and answered the questions before my brother could, which led to more conversation and my pastor praying with me right there in the hallway of our church.

These details are still all I remember from that story, and at around eight years old I must have remembered even less, because as I sat with my friend at her church's Vacation Bible School listening to the same spiel they give every year, my little heart felt full of doubt. It's not as if I thought my parents were lying to me when they had shared that story of what happened five years earlier, but I didn't remember it happening, and oh how my little heart just wanted to remember it happening. I wanted the remembered assurance, I wanted to be able to look back and say "Yes, I know when I became His and this is how it happened." After feeling that little tug assuring me it was okay to step up, I prayed with some lady in the front, filled out my little card, stood in line behind my friend Katie who, until that moment I didn't know had also come up, and handed it to a pastor I had never talked to before and have never seen since.

While, like me, knowing the moment matters to some, but in actuality, knowing the moment doesn't really matter. Each of us will have a different story of when God's love overpowered our sinful flesh and we began to understand that we, on our own, cannot be who we are meant to be, asked to be, or created to be. Whether it happens in childhood, adulthood, or old age; whether it comes with an immediate full-blown understanding of the Gospel of Jesus or through decades of wrestling with the facts makes no difference. Because, even if you remember the experience perfectly, don't recollect a time you were not a Christian, or look back at it all as more of a slow dawning over a lifetime, the moment you become a child of God, through the blood of Christ, is the moment you step into a life of inheritance. You enter a life of hope.

That hope was promised long ago, foreshadowed by the prophets, and then fulfilled so that we would not be left hopeless. Hope was always the plan, and it was the person who would bring it that everyone was waiting for.

In the book of Isaiah, the prophet is dishing out some harsh realities of cities falling apart and destruction reigning over the lives of the ones who inhabit them. I must say that it is quite difficult to read, on an emotional level, when all your focus is on all the tearing down. But when you begin to see the why within it all, your thoughts and emotions start to shift and instead of destruction you see redemption.

In Isaiah 6, as Isaiah hears the voice of the Lord asking who He should send, Isaiah steps up and says, "Here I am. Send Me." Without hesitation, the Lord shares with Isaiah what He wants him to tell all the people. Spoiler alert: It is not a friendly message, but it is one that sets up the entire end game.

> *Go! Say to these people:*
> *Keep listening, but do not understand*
> *Keep looking, but do not perceive.*
> *Make the minds of these people dull;*
> *Deafen their ears and blind their eyes;*
> *Otherwise they might see with their eyes*
> *And hear with their ears,*
> *Understand with their minds,*
> *Turn back and be healed.*
> *Then I (Isaiah) said, "Until when, Lord? And he replied:*
> *Until cities lie in ruins without inhabitants,*
> *Houses are without people,*
> *The land is ruined and desolate,*
> *And the Lord drives the people far away,*
> *Leaving great emptiness in the land.*
> *Though a tenth will remain in the land,*
> *It will be burned again,*
> *Like the terebinth or the oak*
> *that leaves a stump when felled,*
> *the holy seed is the stump.*
> *—Isaiah 6:9-13 (CSB)*

Did you get that last line? The Holy Seed is the stump.

As harsh as it may seem at first glance, the plan is often destruction, or if these semantics sit better with you, a deconstruction of sorts. You are a home with raw potential, and covering you up with paint is not going to cut it. Walls need to come down because, like Chip Gaines says, it's Demo Day! The pruning, the refining, the sometimes destroying until all that is left is a stump is necessary and when that lone stump is the holy seed, the most amazing and beautiful things are built upon it.

The bomb that blew up how my marriage was functioning also blew up my insecurities, blew up deep-rooted sin in my heart, and blew up the idols I put before Him. My God, in all His violent love and wisdom, blew my life apart for one purpose: so that He could rebuild it the way He wanted it to be, the way I needed it to be. He needed to build a life set on the hope of His promises, and not on the things I tried to do myself, not on the things that just ended up blocking the way.

I can look back at that moment and remember where the journey started, but until my life on Earth is done, the race will continue to be run. From that first (and second) meeting of my heart with His, almost thirty years have passed, and countless mistakes, missteps, and downright stupidity have occurred as I have walked through this life. But knowledge, wisdom, and forgiveness have overwhelmed my flesh consistently, because while I am sinful, I am also covered in Christ's blood, and His Spirit is forever at work within me and forever will be. That Holy Stump that was left? That cornerstone on which all else is built? That is hope.

Hope is the excited anticipation of the future, yet certain, blessing of God's grace.

Hope is the ability for you and me to live in our present

state, whatever it may be, expecting and anticipating the future to come because of what Jesus has done for us in the past. Unshaken in the present, hopeful for the future, because of the past.

Hope is available because of Jesus. Hope was brought by Jesus. Jesus was the Hope of the world and still is, through His Spirit, with us in the world. Therefore, when we think about having Hope we can think of having the Person of Christ with us, right there, firm and secure.

In the midst of the distress felt in the book of Jeremiah when the Israelites are being exiled to Babylon under a new ruler, God throws out the encouraging words that now grace many a farmhouse-style sign. "'For I know the plans I have for you,' declares the LORD, 'plans to prosper you and not to harm you, plans to give you a hope and a future.'" (Jeremiah 29:11, NIV) That plan, that Hope, that future was the life and work of Jesus. That grace that exists that we can excitedly anticipate in our future is the Hope that comes through Christ.

The reason the world changed the meaning of hope to nothing more than a fleeting wish is because through their own limited view they looked at the state of man and that of the world around them and thought hope must be bad because they never got anything "good" when they wanted it. Therefore, hope is a let-down and a tease, "delayed disappointment" as was so sadly stated. It has been reduced to nothing more than that wish you throw out that might be a winning ticket for one while millions of others are disappointed.

With God removed from the scenario, with the true Hope of the world forgotten, theirs is the only conclusion left to find. A life without God IS hopeless. It is a life with nothing lasting to hang on to. But real hope, biblical, divinely and originally created hope, is the most secure and comforting place you can be.

Hope is not a maybe. It is not a fleeting wish. It is excitedly anticipating the fulfillment of God's future blessing for you, His child, while living this side of heaven. It is knowing that we are guaranteed a life of grace because of what our Savior did when He sacrificed Himself for us. Hope entered the inner place behind the curtain and became for us the sure and steadfast anchor of our soul.

Hope, true hope, is unfailing. Hope in God's promises will remain with you through the next thing and the next thing and the next, pouring into your heart, building up your faith, and drawing you into deeper relationship with Him. It is beauty given to us. But in bomb-exploding life-pausers, in those hardest experiences we face, it can feel unreachable, so we must learn how to see it always, notice it always, because there is always hope. And there is always hope because there is always Jesus.

To truly rest right there in the hope provided, to truly see and understand the hope that has been given freely through Jesus, we must first trust that it is true. We must see that God's promises are real and not like those of man. We must see what a promise truly means and how God is the ultimate promise keeper.

One of the most difficult things in walking with God or with making the decision to even trust God to begin with is remembering to not see or look at Him as we see and look at ourselves and others. We have the tendency to take this Creator of all things and shrink Him down to human size where we stare at Him, think of Him, and expect of Him what we would expect of the imperfect beings we tangibly walk around with on a daily basis.

While there are beautiful souls that walk this earth who shine the light of Christ in our midst, our hearts have been hurt by other people, our trust has been betrayed by other people, our lives have held surprises that do not bring happy smiles as a result of the choices of other people. Lest we think we are innocent, this array of not-so-wonderfulness pales in comparison to the mistakes and hurt we have caused others and ourselves as well.

Because of these experiences and these choices, we are often tempted and sometimes fall prey to putting God in a flawed people suit, diminishing His divinity and imperishable perfection. It is these failed interactions with other people that have twisted our understanding of promise and produced doubt in our belief that there are promises that exist that are unbreakable.

I have broken many promises. While more than a few exist that I fully intended to keep only to have life derail my ability, plenty of those promises I made I never intended to keep. In fact, the moment the words *I promise* came out of my mouth, my mind knew I was not planning on making good on the rest of the sentence—sometimes because I was not capable of it, but often because I did not have the desire to do so.

We make promises for an array of reasons. The well-intentioned ones are to bring joy to the life of another, to help another through a hard time, and to show others that we love them through our words and deeds. But, on the other side, we also make promises to twist situations in our favor, appease another for a moment, and, quite frankly, to get ourselves out of trouble. In the world of parenting, or in my personal parenting world, hearing the words *I promise* are a giant red flag that the blond boy in question one hundred percent did not do what he is promising he did or that he one hundred percent did what he is promising he didn't.

With all of this happening, it makes sense to have doubts in the promises of others, to wait it out and test the waters to see if their word really is their bond. Also, on the other side, it's understandable that if you have broken your own promises to another many times that you need to build up that trust again before they will, once more, take you at your word.

But God has never broken a promise, has never proven himself unworthy of our praise, and even in the midst of shuffling through the collateral damage of the biggest bomb-exploding circumstance, there is nothing He has promised that He has not produced.

If you take the Word of God given to us through Scripture and travel through the Old Testament prophecies, through reading after reading of people and places that served their purpose in the story that leads up to Christ, you will be struck more than ever by the promises of God. Each prophecy, those words uttered for centuries from the mouths of prophets to His people on earth, were promises. They were words told long ago of what God promised for the future.

From the beginning with the promises He made Adam and Eve about what would happen if they ate from that cursed tree, to the land and inheritance He promised to Abraham, to the release He promised the Israelites from their captors, and to the protection He promised them again when they were sent into exile in Babylon, you see His words fulfilled. Chapter after chapter, sentence after sentence, story after story, God's words are laid out and His promises are spoken and satisfied.

The beautiful words the angels said when they appeared to Zechariah, Elizabeth, Mary, and Joseph were promises of children to come. One of those children paved the way of the Lord and the other was our Lord, sent to earth to take on the sins of man, which was the ultimate fulfillment of those promises spoken through the prophets. Jesus is the ultimate fulfillment of the very hope we are learning to fully trust and hold on to. But if we want to dig even deeper into the amazing story the whole of the Bible tells, we see that Jesus was actually more than a kept promise; He was what secured the promise.

In Leviticus we are introduced to a word more substantial than promise: *covenant.* This specific covenant is one that God made with His people. When you read through Leviticus 26 (I'll wait right here if you want to do that really quickly), you see this covenant of the Old Testament laid out with the promises of what will happen if we keep His commands and follow His decrees. Peace, power over enemies, having favor and multiplying are but a few, but the greatest of all is God's intention to walk among us, to be our God and have us be His people.

Even later in the chapter when we are confronted with the punishment for disobeying His commands and not following His decrees, which we all will inevitably do, amongst the not-so-fun list of consequences is the statement that even though we will fail, if we confess our sins, He will still remember His covenant with His people. (Leviticus 26:40-42) But even with the glimmer of hope that comes as you read of the despair brought on by disobedience, remember there is always hope, because better yet, so much better yet, is the news that with one life that covenant has been kept once and for all.

In Hebrews 8:8–12, we are told of a new covenant.

> *"The days are coming, declares the Lord,*
> *when I will make a new covenant*

with the people of Israel
and with the people of Judah.
It will not be like the covenant
I made with their ancestors
when I took them by the hand
to lead them out of Egypt,
because they did not remain faithful to my covenant,
and I turned away from them,
declares the Lord.
This is the covenant I will establish with the people of Israel
after that time, declares the Lord.
I will put my laws in their minds
and write them on their hearts.
I will be their God,
and they will be my people.
No longer will they teach their neighbor,
or say to one another, 'Know the Lord,'
because they will all know me,
from the least of them to the greatest.
For I will forgive their wickedness
and will remember their sins no more." (NIV)

"The new covenant is established on better promises," we are also told in this chapter of Hebrews, because it is established through Christ, the one who secured all promises for us with His life, death, and resurrection. And just as God promised at the end of that litany of dread in the conclusion of Leviticus 26, He did dwell among us through His Son being made flesh, and He does still dwell among us as His Son sent His Spirit down as a helper to his children. More promises fulfilled.

Every single word God spoke or left with us in His Word

was a promise of what will come, what He will do, and of who He is, and not once in all of time has He broken any of those promises. In fact, this great Covenant Keeper went a step further and secured them for us once and for all with Christ. That covenant is the relational emphasis to the overwhelming number of promises.

No, the way His promises are fulfilled did not and still do not always happen in the ways our minds can imagine or even comprehend. God reminds us, again through Isaiah, that our thoughts are not His thoughts and our ways are not His ways. His thoughts are higher. His ways are higher. All the rain and snow that is coming down on the earth upsetting our plans and causing floods and annoyance, He is using it to water and cause growth so that it can accomplish in us what He needs it to. From it will not come briars and thorns, but instead trees that stand tall and can be seen from afar and will be everlasting.

Even Jesus, who was perfectly dependent on His Father, who was perfectly in tune with God's will, whose prayer life kept him in direct contact to fulfill His Father's plan, even He Himself prayed in the Garden of Gethsemane on the night of His arrest that, if it was possible, the cup would be taken from Him. But just because we would choose a different way, an easier way, to fulfill the promise does not mean that God ever broke His, and like Jesus on that same night, sometimes our only response can be "not my will but Yours be done." (Matthew 26:39) Jesus never doubted that God's promise was true, but in His humanity He showed us that He understood the hard that comes sometimes for God's promises to be accomplished.

God sees the big picture. He has the ultimate view of the complete and finished story. He can see the beauty that is being created all around the yuck, and though He never promised it would be easy, He did promise us a Savior. That Savior gave us His Spirit to dwell within us, thus proving that, just as Scripture says, He will never leave you or forsake you (Joshua 1:5), He will be faithful to complete the work began in you (Philippians 1:6), all of this will work out for good (Romans 8:28), and that you have nothing to fear. (Isaiah 41:10)

Far better than even the most well-intentioned promises I make my baby boys, and the most genuine love I attempt to heap upon them, is the comfort of a Heavenly Father who knows no end, and the promises He has made that can never be broken.

It was these promises, this covenant, and their fulfillment that brought hope into the world. Hope is the excited anticipation of the future yet certain blessing of God's grace. But our hearts can become heavy and our minds swayed, and with each bomb in life these truths we may know so well can't seem to be grasped. There are times when hope is not our immediate reaction, when something else is instead. What do we do then? Have we failed? Have we lost? No, of course not; but we do need to learn. We need to learn how to search for hope, how to find hope in each and every situation. And sometimes, before we cling again to the hope we have found, we need to start in a place of hopelessness.

3

Hopeless

My church had always been a place of refuge, a place that brought joy, a place to huddle up before emerging out into the world for another week carrying the truth learned with you. Housed in that little building in the middle of a strip mall were the people who knew me, loved me, held my babies at the hospital and again on Sunday mornings so that this mama could sit and rest, not just physically, but spiritually, as the words soaked in with no distractions.

But now it is different, and that church is no longer a place of peace, but a reminder of a life that has changed, a life that is bearing a brand new wound that hasn't even had time to build up the protection of a scab, let alone heal with the glimpse of a scar. In every glance, from the parking lot and within, is a minefield of mental triggers as I figure out how to navigate the small hallways, knowing it's not if I will run into her, but when, and how I will respond when I do.

What will happen this time? Will I feel at home? Or will the betrayal be made new? My feelings and fears are constantly changing. When one area of life experiences improvement it's often at the cost of another, or at least that is how it feels as it all plays out. My heart hurts. My stomach hurts. My brain hurts. Too much thinking, too much processing; how much can one person take in such a short peri-od? Surely there will be another explosion in my heart just from the aftermath left from the original one. Do bombs have aftershocks like earthquakes do, or is this just the shrapnel embedded within that has not been found and removed, inching its way closer to my heart ready to take aim?

The boys bound out of the car in all their childhood exuberance, excited to see friends, as I sit wiping away the tears that are spilling regardless of how much mental energy is being used to force them not to appear. Giving myself yet another pep talk and praying yet another prayer that I can survive the morning, I have the courage to get out of the car.

Deep breath. Open door. Walk in . . .

I can't stand at the edge of the pool in our backyard and jump straight in, let alone run through the gate and just leap without looking. I have to ease in, testing the waters as I go, until I fully submerge. The more I am need of cooling off, the quicker the process goes, but no matter the timeline, first I have to feel the heat so that I can not just appreciate the cool, but also seek it out.

Likewise, before you can rest in the infinite hope our Creator brings, you must find yourself in a place of hopelessness or, at the very least, come to the realization that hopelessness does exist, even if only for a moment.

Talking about hope without talking about hopelessness makes no sense. When dealing with opposites, it's essential to acknowledge both. Usually the very definition of one is used to define the other. If one did not exist, the other wouldn't need to. If hopelessness wasn't with us, if it wasn't a prevalent part of life on this earth, hope wouldn't be necessary.

Quenching thirst comes from feeling thirsty, seeking rest comes from feeling tired, and a source of strength is needed when you feel weak. You find something because you realize it was lost. You look for hope when you see that without it you are completely hopeless.

I hate to be the bearer of bad news, but this looking for hope is not a one-time sightseeing trip. Of course, come to think of it, that's actually the best news because it means that hopelessness, like other things, happens. It's not a rarity. It's not bad luck or the statistic of a disease that only affects the smallest margin. It's common, and while that doesn't seem reassuring at first, as you let that sink in, the realization comes that you are not alone; the walk from hopelessness to hope is a well-worn path for us all. Comfort can then come through experiencing that even though the road is well-trodden, the pace will eventually quicken as you learn the way out.

I spent many years thinking that my Christian walk must be a task of building knowledge upon knowledge until finished before me was a high-rise with clean and sparkling windows large enough for the world to see, ready to welcome in others and produce its work, proving to all what a good job it could do.

Instead, over the years, I have seen that my Christian walk is more like a parking lot. Widespread, it stretches out, busier at times than others depending on the time of day or time of year. Remainders of old lines have faded away, memories of others have been covered over as the new spaces were drawn, and the occasional pothole scattered around just won't seem to stay filled in no matter how many times workers complete the task. While not as glamorous as a pinnacle in a skyline, parking lots are not so bad; they humbly provide rest, bearing the burden of others going about their daily errands.

This different understanding was not just a mental shift caused by a different light bulb going off all of a sudden. And those years referenced in which a new understanding took place all reside on the post-bomb side of life. It was the outcome of a lot of misunderstood truths and a wobbly self-built tower being blown to bits. Nothing in my life was left untouched. And thank God for it. His new work was an extensive work. He leaves no stone unturned.

Before, after searching through my dust-filled memory banks, I became aware of my previous process for the sky-scraper attempts at spiritual growth. I gathered stories and lessons beginning from childhood Sunday school that told of rights and wrongs, of which characters did what, and of how it worked out for them in the end. I also watched others around me like an eagle in an attempt to pinpoint their mistakes, not to throw them back at them, but to learn from them so that I wouldn't make the same ones myself. I read books, including the Bible, to garner words of advice, instruction, and correction. Then I took all of these things and attempted to build a single tower of correct work and achievement.

We aren't meant to build skyscrapers of praise to ourselves in an attempt to show off all we have accomplished or even in an attempt to show off all God has accomplished in us. The people of Israel tried that once and it definitely did not work out the way they were planning. In Genesis 11: 1–8, they looked at each other, in all of their sameness (same looks, same views, same language), and said to each other, "Let's build ourselves a city, with a tower that reaches to the heavens, so that we can make a name for ourselves, because if we don't, we might be scattered over the whole earth." (NIV)

Well, a name was certainly made, and that name was Babel, because God, needing to keep them from self-destructing, created different languages, separated His people, and scattered them around the world where they continued to grow and spread out, not up. You see, parking lots are indeed a much better plan.

Why Hopelessness Is a First Reaction

In the story of the Tower of Babel, their worst nightmare was to be scattered, and in the end their worst nightmare came true. Whether or not they ever saw the good that came later because of it, at that moment they found themselves confused, lost, and yes, hopeless.

Pastor and church planter David Crandall explains suffering as a reaction to when something you are putting your hope in is taken away. Hopelessness is a product of suffering. We will experience unpleasant things on our own or will even be subjected to them by another. In real talk, things are going to happen that simply stink, whether they are our fault or not. There will be loss. Something will be taken away, be it a job, a relationship, a life, or even an intangible thing such as a lifelong dream or your reputation. In the midst of that experience, whatever it is, we become hopeless if that thing that held all of our hope is lost, because without it we do not know where to turn.

When this takes place, in our own brilliant, flawed wisdom we attempt to solve this problem in such a way that next time we'll avoid hopelessness. To do so, we reorganize, we try to get smart and not put all our hope in one thing. We diversify our emotional economy. Instead of heaping all the hope in a single place, we spread our hope around to multiple places whether, again, it be a job, a relationship, a goal, etc. That way, we think if we just lose one, the loss won't be as great and then, logically, the suffering will not be as great, thus lessening the feeling of hopelessness. We are often too smart for our own good.

When we place hope—in small amounts or great—in what can be lost, we never had true hope to begin with. Furthermore, if placing our hope in things that can be lost means that you never had true hope, then one could also argue that we were always hope-less and therefore that lack of hope requires hopelessness to be our first reaction to everything unless we know in whom true hope is found.

There is only one source of hope, the person of Christ. He brought Hope into the world and all hope must rest on him. Why? Because He is the only source that cannot be taken away or lost. He is the only person who will not leave or abandon us. His death on the cross gained us eternal forgiveness and his resurrection from the dead gave us eternal life with Him. That new covenant which was made cannot be broken, will not be broken.

But why does hopelessness still happen? Why, when even if we do know Jesus, do we find ourselves shaken, souls screaming for answers? Because we are running the race. We are not finished yet. Knowledge may be gained in a moment, but wisdom requires a well-fought battle to achieve. Life is full of continuous change, small steps forward, bigger steps back, then jumps and loops and ladders and circles and slides and—well, you get the picture.

Sanctification is a process. Yes, you are justified, made right before God, in that immediate moment you surrendered your life to be hidden in Christ's, but God is not a fairy godmother.

He does not wave His wand and transform what everyone else sees, what you see. He changed your heart from stone to flesh in a moment, but the rest requires a bit more time. Not because He isn't capable of the immediate, but because for your good and His glory we must walk the walk of faith while you are walking here on earth.

So, great, it's a process. Got it. But how does the process work? How do we go from point A of hopelessness to point B of resting in true, biblical hope? And how long will it take?

When it comes down to it, in those first moments of a struggle, a new hard thing or an old one that has resurfaced once again, my greatest desire would be to be able to tell you that the first thing I do is cling to the One that gives true hope, especially since I'm writing a book on it. But, alas, the reason this book needs to be written is because usually the opposite occurs. Because I have again placed my hope in something that can be lost, usually the contentment that comes from a period of calm circumstances, I fall prey to the feeling of hopelessness. Instead of hopeful and trusting, I am like the fearful ant in *A Bug's Life* whose path has suddenly been obstructed. Instead of calmly searching out where to go next I am in the field screaming "I'm Lost! Where's the line? It just went away. What do I do? We'll be stuck here forever!"[10]

Dramatic, yes. Truthful, all the yeses. And in full disclosure, I hated it about myself. I hated that the hope I thought I had disappeared so quickly. I hated that when I thought I had a firm grasp on Jesus it turned out that I was holding on to something else instead. I hated that feeling that I had misunderstood, misjudged, or just straight missed the boat. Hated it until my personal truths were blown to pieces to reveal the real ones, the Ones that can never be destroyed.

For many years I thought that feeling hopeless was just a sign that one had given over to a sin hiding inside. That, yet again, I had failed, in some way, to trust, and that nagging hopeless feeling was my punishment, the manifestation of a job decidedly not "well done, good and faithful servant."

The weeks leading up to the detonation of the particular life bomb that initiated, inspired, and/or required the searching for true hope were in fact full of hopeless feelings. As life seemed just not right, as conversations with my husband always resulted in hurt feelings or frustrations, as encounters with my friend always felt strained or awkward or less than genuine, I struggled with feeling hopeless because I did not understand why my relationships were failing, or at least feeling very sub-par. The feelings of anger, resentment, jealousy, and frustration welling up inside just fueled that hopeless feeling as I misread the emotion and assumed that it was my sin of not being a good enough wife or a good enough friend or a good enough anything that was causing it all. Then the bomb. And from the bomb there came through the gift of grace, clarity.

I know now that hopelessness is not a punishment; hopelessness is an arrow. It's a dart that directs you to your heart in order to see what is causing the struggle that keeps you up, changes your attitude, and creeps, if left to itself, into every aspect of your life. Hopelessness is used to point us straight to hope.

Those feelings of hopelessness were meant to send me to Jesus. They were meant to overwhelm my earthly senses so that the only thing left to lean on was my spiritual sense, the Holy Spirit residing in me gifted by Jesus as my helper, my guide, my untainted-by-sin wisdom. Understanding hopelessness in this way doesn't necessarily keep it from rearing its head less often, but it does direct us to the hope that is always there and, in effect, hold at bay the swarms of negatives like I was experiencing that can potentially come in the wake of hopelessness.

NEGATIVES PRODUCED BY HOPELESSNESS

Just the other day, while standing in the kitchen looking at the piles of recently purchased school supplies all sorted for each child and feeling exhausted from a day of running all the errands, all while dwelling on the fact that the state of a summer-filled house is more than a little overwhelming to think about putting back in order, I noticed that the inside edge of our back door was disgustingly dirty.

"How," I asked out loud in a huff of frustration, "does part of a door that no one touches get that filthy?"

My overhearing husband's response was, "Isn't it interesting that when anything in the world is left to its own devices, it goes downhill instead of getting better?"

We forget. We leave things alone for too long. We place some things above others on the to-do list and thus the caretaking suffers, leaving us vulnerable, not on our guard, and not resting in the One who guards us. In the absence of this focus, when the Spirit drives us toward the very thing that we need, our flesh sends us down in the opposite direction, and instead of living in hope we convince ourselves that all is hopeless.

Hopelessness can be a scary feeling. It reminds us of our loss of control or, truth be known, of our never having had control to begin with. Of all the negative emotions I can think of—fear, anxiety, humiliation, sadness, etc.—hopelessness can be the worst of all.

The reason for this is simple: if you have the wrong idea of hopelessness, if you do not recognize it as a gift that points our hearts up, it instead becomes a cancer that feeds itself and grows, convincing each emotion you have that it should take the same ugly, hopeless road toward the darkness instead of toward the light.

Negativity feeds negativity, like a domino effect that cannot be stopped without, as Newton proved, an equal and opposite reaction. There are four specific negatives that hopelessness have the potential to generate in the midst of one of life's difficult situations, and like that slippery slope, you can quickly find yourself starting at the top of the first and sliding all the way to rock bottom.

First, the unguarded side of hopelessness will do its best to convince you that it's not just the situation that's the problem, it's you. In a word, this side of hopelessness can produce within you a feeling of **shame**. Shame is defined as "a painful feeling of humiliation or distress caused by the consciousness of wrong or foolish behavior."[11] Distress is just another word for hopelessness. Within distress you feel stuck, unable to find a way out.

Let's be honest though, you are going to behave wrongly and foolishly. You just are. That marathon we mentioned is still going on, your running shoes are still tied tight and the finish line is a ways away. Foolish and wrong behavior is part of the package dating back to the first sin committed in the garden. Sanctification is a process that winds its way through sin and repentance, but just because sin is present does not mean shame must follow.

Researcher and author Brené Brown tells us, "Shame corrodes the very part of us that believes we are capable of change."[12] The unguarded side of hopelessness will use the weapon of shame to hide from you the comfort and forgiveness of hope, the hope that tells us that we, through Christ, are not just capable of change, but have already been changed.

No matter the cause, the choice, or the wrongdoing you took part in, YOU are not a problem. You may have one, to be sure (a plateful sits in front of me), and it is a surety that you have more than enough on your own plate as well. We are not innocent; Romans 3:23 tells us that we have all fallen short. Within these short fallings, we may make a single choice or a whole string of choices that cause consequences and hurts for ourselves and others. But hope tells us that even though there are consequences for every choice that we make, losing the love of God is never one of them.

Romans 5:8 reminds us that "God showed his love for us in that while we were still sinners, Christ died for us." (ESV) He didn't send His son to die for us when we were problem-free but when we were chock full of them—not to condemn us, but to save us. Hopelessness, that feeling of being lost, should point us to the One who finds. But with that kind and talented Dr. Jekyll (hope) can come the wicked and violent Mr. Hyde (unguarded hopelessness).

Hopelessness in its ugliest state will convince you that you are worthless. And there are times that this feeling of shame will temporarily win you over. It will succeed in convincing you that you mean nothing to anyone, that whom you are and what you have done is so terrible or so ugly or so imperfect that there is nothing left for you. With this belief comes yet another onslaught of emotion: bitterness, anger, callousness, and depression, just to name a few.

When shame stays planted instead of being uprooted, when

hopelessness does not point you up to Hope but brings you down instead, it will eat at your heart, mind, and soul and cause the next slip, the next negative: **the retreat**.

When my oldest was around the age of two, in his Easter basket was a huge plastic egg full of Starbursts, his absolute favorite candy. Unbeknownst to me, he begged his daddy to let him take the egg to bed with him with the promise that he wouldn't eat them but would just look at them. Permission was granted and that little boy set a great temptation right alongside his head as he attempted to rest. The next day, after his nap, that son came out feeling terrible and my mama heart broke as I laid him on the couch and went back to his room to fetch his favorite blanket and bear. As I straightened his bed before coming back in with them, my eye caught a glimpse of paper peeking out from under his pillow and a quick check revealed thirty-plus candy wrappers in a pile, hidden.

We may show off our successes from every mountain we can find to make sure others see what we are capable of or how much we deserve the blessings or reward given, but our failures, or I should say those things we think to be failures, we hide, stuffing them under a pillow so others cannot see. When our minds are full of mistakes and "unwanteds," we retreat, hiding our faces from public view, thinking we can also hide our hearts. Like Adam and Eve huddled behind bushes in the garden, we desire to keep ourselves from the ones who know us, the ones we know if given the chance won't just see, but really SEE.

When hopelessness lets shame overrule, we feel we must protect ourselves from the truth instead of abiding in it. So we sit, declining invitations to see friends, being absent with our spouses or children, staring at unopened Bibles, filling our time with social media and the like, making any excuse to seclude ourselves, all the while waiting for the day those problems or feelings will disappear so that we can again walk proudly into the light, because then we will be okay with what others can see. But did time really heal those wounds or did it give us the opportunity to stuff them under the pillow, deeper this time so that they were better hidden, never to be found?

However, being a recluse or hermit or "off the grid," or whatever term is socially acceptable for one who wishes to remain apart from the presence of others, is much more difficult than you may think. So, as much as we may like to play the part of the ostrich, most times hiding is just impossible, or at least hiding for the amount of time we deem necessary for everything to go back as it should. Absence is impractical because there are too many responsibilities, too many people who would notice, too many questions that could be asked. So if hiding won't work, we must slip down to the next level: putting up **a false front**.

If a wrong view of hopelessness can eat away at the inside of you where the light cannot touch it, consider what it could do on the outside, much like the obvious infection of a wound or rot in a piece of lumber. One would think if all of those thoughts and feelings of shame stemming from a wrong view of hopelessness were going on inside your heart and mind, your outward self would reveal it, whether through actions toward others, demeanor and countenance, the words you say, or a combination of all. Something would show, should show, and then just observing someone's behavior—friend or foe, stranger or neighbor—would give a gauge of their feelings and therefore a sense of how they are doing in this life. Unfortunately, most often, that's not what happens.

When hiding alone is not an option, we instead hide in plain sight. Lest you think you are too intelligent to let someone pull this emotional fast one on you, think again.

Not long after beginning the focus on forgiving, healing, and rebuilding after our personal life bomb, I was in need of a little time away for both marriage and sanity's sake so I tagged along on a trip to Las Vegas where my husband was presenting at a conference. Let's be honest, sending him to Vegas alone would have just been a stupid idea in the wake of everything, and it was going to be good for both of us to be together without the kids and for me to lay by a pool in the sun for a week to escape from the ongoing processing of the revealed situation. Oh, the non-stop processing.

Three days of lying in my self-prescribed sun went by before I noticed a fluttering above my eye line and, after staring a bit longer than usual, I saw that the beautiful hotel wall that loomed over me was nothing more than a piece of fabric imprinted with the meticulous details of the stone-carved window encasements that surrounded me on the other side of the solidly built exteriors. This facade was even complete with the glare marks that would have appeared on the pristinely clean glass. My eyes had deceived me all along; it took the outside source of wind power to reveal what had been right in front of me.

Knowing how someone is doing and what they are feeling by merely observing rarely reveals the truth. Even if you are closer to that person than anyone and are asking all the right questions, their true heart could still not be what you're getting, or if we're the ones in distress, what we're giving.

We know how to fake it. To be frank, we are experts at faking it.

As you become an adult you develop and fine tune the

qualities your parents tried to teach you, like self-control, using polite phrases, basic manners, small talk, etc. Those are all good things and can certainly make you a more desirable person to be around; however, like all good things, they can be twisted just a hair and become a detriment to your heart. When you are skilled at proper etiquette or honestly just skilled at not coming off as a jerk, then you are skilled in the art of hiding in plain sight.

With little to no effort, depending on how many situations we have practiced this in, we're able to fool those around us by using our words and actions to mask our hearts, all with the intention of hiding the hopelessness within us. Even if everything inside us is screaming to just say what we are really feeling, taking that step of letting it show is one that seems just a bit impossible. Instead, we put all our energy into appearing ok, as if nothing is wrong in the least, and when succeeding in making others believe it, we attempt to believe it ourselves.

Fake it 'til you make it isn't a bad policy to have when taking on a new job or learning a new talent, but, in the case of masking that hopelessness within, it can be damaging. Putting up that facade is really just building a lie. It's the intent to make what others see look perfectly put together in order to keep them off the scent of your distress and keep you from having to talk about whatever it is that is distressing. At some point, to keep the facade going, you yourself will have to begin to believe it and will inevitably slide down to the last negative on the slope and begin **lying to yourself**.

Think back to that moment during the holiday season when you were sitting around the table with family late at night after all the kids are in bed, when you can finally have an adult conversation, or at least a conversation with only other adults. As the conversation carries on and memories are being shared, you tell a story only to have a sibling look at you in disbelief and inform you the particular event didn't happen to you but to them! You've been telling that story for years, YEARS. Mind blown, you sit in confusion. How could this be?

Say it enough times and in your mind it becomes truth. You have woven a tale so familiar that it must be real, and you remember so effortlessly that it must be factual. Your brain took the information and built a new pathway, so how can you go back again?

If you let hopelessness take over your emotions instead of letting it point you to truth, you begin to live life based on a lie. Just like sin itself began with a lie, this hopelessness begins and ends with one as well. That lie is that you should live in shame, that you must hide yourself, that you must put a fake front out for others, which then forces you to lie to yourself about what the original truth is.

Ultimately, the lie is that there is no hope. But, as we know, there is always hope.

The realization that those hopeless feelings were not a curse, but a path toward saving, was a balm that began the process of healing my soul. When we see what can happen when hopelessness is misunderstood, when we let it guide us to shame instead of point us to hope, it changes everything. But that understanding, that realization, is not capable without recognition, without seeing the feelings for what they really are. Admission of need is the first step of recovery, but before we recognize our need for hope we must learn to recognize the feelings of hopelessness that can be used to point us to it.

RECOGNIZING THE EMOTION OF HOPELESSNESS

So, how do we define *hopelessness?* How do we know it when we see it, not just in others, because in that we like to think we are all somewhat more astute, but in ourselves? How can we take notice so that later we can call it out and even later we can let hope take its place?

In simple terms, hopelessness means to be without hope, but it manifests itself in a myriad of ways in innumerable lives. When asked in a survey to share words or feelings that come to mind when hearing the word *hopeless,* these were some responses:

- "Stuck. Shame. Pointless."
- "Despair. Sadness. Lost."
- "Despair. Agony. Helplessness. Over. Death. Suicide."
- "Fear of what's ahead."
- "Lost."
- "Broken. Rock-bottom. What's next."
- "Depression. Paralysis."
- "Stuck in a place that's impossible to get out of. Desperate. Despairing. Down in the bottom with nowhere else to go and no one to turn to."

These words are too heavy and these feelings carry too much weight to be cast aside, to not be addressed. These emotions demand relief. Lives depend on it.

The problem with hopelessness is that it's easy to define after the fact, easy to see in hindsight; but in the middle, in the trenches of the feeling, it can become lost in the scenery of set and determined eyes and result in just another hill to climb, another problem to solve, another failure to bear the brunt of.

All seems clear in our lives when we are on a mountaintop

and even still in the times when we are walking on level ground, but the moment we begin slipping into a downward spiral isn't always as noticeable. As shared earlier, traumatic things, bombs as we've been describing them, can come in a moment, whether they're the result of our choices or not. And we can take the next steps without even noticing, at first, the empty space that is under our feet.

We've already covered opposites and their need to be to-gether to define one another, to understand one another. On its positive side, hopelessness informs us that something is wrong, something is not as it should be. Help must come. That help is hope.

The way of recognizing hopelessness when it appears is by knowing what hope is, and by letting hope guide the way.

There's a reason why most of the time we hit rock bottom, we hit it before we look up. Before we're at the bottom there are still deeper places to try on our own before we see the need of another way. In the process of tackling what comes at us, we miss that what we are really doing is pushing things away. Initially it seems as if the goal would be for us all to recognize the feelings in the middle of the fall instead of at the bottom in order to catch ourselves on the way down, to stick our arms and feet out to brace our bodies against the walls and then start the climb back up and out. But you can't climb up on your own, you never could, even if it feels like you have done it be-fore. The real escape from the bottom can only come through Christ.

Remember, we will fall, we will be foolish. There may be times that the feelings of hopelessness come up and you will immediately be able to let them point you to hope, but there will be other times when you will slip all the way down; the only difference is that when you know hope, when you have Jesus as that assurance, you may sit in hopelessness for a time but, you will never stay.

When you know hope, instead of dwelling in the hopelessness, you will have the ability to have your eyes turned upward, to its opposite, to the place where hope is found. With hope you can recognize hopelessness, and with hope that hopelessness can be used for good. But this is only possible if that truth is living within you. The problem comes when you have never known true hope. Without hope, your only option is to be hopeless. If you have always lived your life in the dark, you haven't the faintest clue was light is like. Darkness can be your only option.

There is only one true light and it came down to us from heaven, gifted to us. In John 1:5, Jesus said, "I am the light of the world. Whoever follows me will never walk in darkness, but will have the light of life." (ESV) It doesn't stop there, because when we follow the light, the light of Hope, and when we understand that this same Hope can be present within us, we too can be a light. Because we are promised with him in Matthew 5:14 that we are "a light of the world. A city on a hill that cannot be hidden!" (ESV)

Hope is there to cling to when we are required by life to cling, and it is also there to wrap its arms around us when we can't hold on any longer. Life with God doesn't mean stepping into a life of easy perfection where everything goes your way and you no longer have a care in the world. Life with God means your cares grow bigger, your feelings for them stronger, and the difficulties that come from caring more frequent. Life with God means you are living this life with all its ups and downs, resting in the promise of the good hope God provides.

Let's learn to not just recognize hopelessness, but also learn to see hope. Let's search hope out, discover where to find it, what may block it from our view, and then how to reach out and cling to it. Most importantly, let's learn that when you inevitably let go, it never lets go of you.

4

Blockers of Hope

My friend had just had a baby. Sitting in her house, with her arms full of joy and sleeplessness, she waited for the home-cooked dinner that was on my back seat. I drove around her neighborhood for a good long time before I finally willed the car to stop in front of her house. The thing was, she didn't know yet about what I was going through in my own life, and I didn't know how to tell her. How do you share this kind of news with someone so full with the newness of a little life created with love? I needed more time. More time to build up a script in my head of how to share information about our situation with those who weren't a part of the bomb squad. When you see a bomb go off, no one has to tell you what happened or even that it happened. But all those other people, the ones who weren't there to view it or who weren't within earshot, have to find out some way.

I didn't want hearsay, I didn't want groups huddled in corners, I didn't want the evening news. I wanted it from my mouth to the ears of the ones I loved. I wanted to be able to explain and soften what could possibly come out harsh, but I was scared. Scared of the response, scared of the reaction, scared of the snap judgments or typical assumptions, scared that I wouldn't be able to get through the first sentence without succumbing to the kind of ugly tears that take away your ability to speak and breathe. So, I let fear win. I took a deep breath, counted to ten, took the freshly-baked meal out of the backseat, plastered on a happy smile, knocked on the door, and with all my might lied to my friend for an hour.

What I didn't know then was that that lie would continue for months. My inability to give just a bit of my heart at that moment would build and build until I had inadvertently, yet totally on purpose, kept this sweet friend in the dark. I created for myself someone I could just be normal with, someone who didn't look at me with eyes that held pity because of what had been done to me, but with it created for myself a place in my life that blocked some of the hope that could have been seen through the love of a sister in Christ . . .

When we go through these difficult, bomb-exploding experiences, or even little frustrating scenarios, clinging to hope is usually not our first course of action. At least it is not mine. No matter how many times God has proven himself faithful, no matter how many times I have unsuccessfully tried things on my own only to feel immediate peace come over me when I finally lay it at His feet instead, no matter how many times I learn that clinging to the hope He provides trumps all other things, it is still not my first step.

This problem is a historical one, and not just in my history, but in the history of people in general.

Early in the Bible, God's people lived a life of slavery in Egypt, as recorded in Exodus 12–16. After generations of suffering and oppression, God sent Moses and used him to deliver His people from the clutches of Pharaoh. Can you imagine it? Finally, for the first time in your life, you felt what it was like to be free. Those who only the day before had complete power over you were now handing you money and jewels and treasures just so you would get out faster and be on your way to the land that so long ago God had promised you, His people.

With God leading you as a pillar of fire at night and a pillar of cloud in the day, you march on knowing, seeing, that He, your God, is with you, and you walk forward in praise. But then you hit water, a sea stretched out in front with the enemy coming up behind, and immediately, for lack of a better term, you lose it.

So, that same God, through Moses, makes the sea split in the middle. He takes massive amounts of water and turns them into walls with a path in between right in front of you to use to walk to safety. Not only were you and all your family and roughly 2.4 million people from the Exodus able to make it to the other side, but the enemy who was in hot pursuit became swallowed up by that same water, giving you a feeling of rest that comes from no longer being chased.

Then, after three days of walking in the wilderness without finding water you finally come across a bitter pool which God makes clean and you are revived, seeing again his faithfulness in taking care of you. But now you get hungry, and instead of resting in hope that the same God who rescued you, guided you through the walls of water safely, and gave you water to drink in the midst of the desert will again take care of you, you again begin to lose it and wish you were back in slavery because at least then you had food.

Does God give up, let you die of hunger? No, food fell from the sky. FROM THE SKY! As you gather it up, He makes sure you know that you must only get enough for today, because tomorrow more will come; He is showing you that He will sustain you day by day.

Any guesses how many followed that command?

A pattern of the people's doubt, God's faithfulness, the people's repentance and trust and back again is forming and continues on throughout the Bible and, to be completely transparent, throughout the life I live. Choosing not to cling to the hope God provides has nothing to do with God and His provision. He has proven himself faithful time and time again and will continue to do so both now and forever, because that is who He is. The problem is us and the things we choose to cling to instead, as well as the things that we let block our way.

We all bring sin into everything we do; we can't help it. The Fall changed man forever; that one moment separated us from God and because of that separation, we needed redemption. Hope is redemption; it's Jesus's sacrifice for us so that we will never let hopelessness drag us down again. But that need for redemption only means that sin is present, that nothing we do is pure and for God alone. Our best efforts are filthy rags. If done on our own, our strongest efforts to seek out hope will fail, and we'll be kept from truly seeing where we desire to look.

Going to the zoo has been one of my favorite things to do with our boys since our oldest was one year old. No matter how many times we go, each trip holds something a little bit different, a unique special moment. Whether a different animal feels like showing off that day or the different temperatures result in enjoying the walking or sitting by the splash pad more, each visit is stamped with its own unique memory.

However, as many children as there are who frequent the zoo daily, not all parts of it are built for a child's size. Fences and walls are necessary for safety, as not much good can come from a wild animal escaping their habitat and wandering around the sidewalks with the spectators, but these same safety measures limit vision. They especially limit the vision of the little people I bring with me. "Mama, pick me up!" is a phrase uttered countless times on those days, and as I get a great work out by hefting one boy after another above the rail so that they can see. It's the view from above that brings the most truth, the one that shows the complete picture, the one we can't always see without assistance.

To be able to embrace the hope that God provides through His Son, you have to get a better view. Only the things the Spirit does through us are pure and holy, and only by following His guidance can you be lifted above the rail to see true hope. We have a part in it though; our part is to realize that we need to be lifted up. My boys could have walked around all day seeing nothing but brown wood posts and a blur of animal fur, but they didn't. They desired to be picked up to see what they knew in their hearts was out there. They wanted the full view.

To realize we need to be lifted up, we must first recognize that our vision is blocked and then see what is getting in our way—what's keeping our hearts from seeing, submitting, and abiding in Him. Next, we need a desire to be picked up. Only when the barriers are no longer there can you clearly see what has always been behind them.

However, we are our own worst enemy, and Satan relishes the chance to turn our vision to ourselves and our desires to our solutions, so that our eyes cannot see the hope that surrounds us. We need to ask to see, we need to ask for truth, because it is those truths that will not only give us a view, but will set us free.

So, what is it that gets in the way? What are we setting up to block the view? What is being thrown up in front of us, keeping our eyes from seeing? What are these blockers of hope?

My father-in-law, a Presbyterian pastor (PCA), taught his children that sin can be traced back to two things: fear and unbelief. Similarly, I believe these blockers of hope can be traced to three main categories: fear, distractions, and idols. Let's see where they go, shall we?

HOW FEAR BLOCKS HOPE

Through the story about not opening up to my friend, you can see that fear kept trying to convince me that my story was something to hide, to keep secret so that relationship could still be present. Fear told me that my story was better left in the dark. Darkness can be the worst place to leave anything.

I know in this world there are individuals who struggle with fear to a debilitating degree who need help that goes way beyond the reminders I can bring. I am not certified to give all the help that those may truly need, but I can stop and pray for that help to come. Will you pause for a moment and join me?

The fear to which I am referring is not a result of mental illness, but a simple result of the sin nature we all have within our hearts. As Paul says in 1 Timothy 1:15, "Jesus came into the world to save sinners, of which I am the foremost." (ESV) And when it comes to fears, I, at times, have been the most fearful one I know.

It still amazes my husband the way fears run around in my mind and connect together like a big, massive, chaotic, Atlanta interstate disaster. I-75, I-85, and Spaghetti Junction have got nothing on the ways my thoughts and fears can get entangled. Come to think of it, I'm actually scared of all three of those roads as well.

Without even trying too hard I came up with this list of personal fears:

Bees
The dark
Talking in front of people
Singing in front of people
Climbing up high places
Looking out from high places
Falling from high places
Drowning
Someone breaking in
My husband getting in a car wreck on the way home from work
Losing my husband or children
Being alone in a large public restroom
Walking in the woods at night (walking anywhere at night)
Going inside a bank instead of the drive-thru
Scary movies (Fun fact: a boyfriend in high school broke up with me over this one!)
Coming across the wrong way in a conversation
Hurting someone's feelings
Making someone mad
Roller coasters
Being misunderstood or misinterpreted
Taking off in an airplane
Crashing in an airplane
Leaving my children behind with no parents

I could keep going, but I'll just leave it at that.

Fear comes when we do not trust that things will stay, when we are afraid something we have will disappear. When I look at my list, it's easy to see the basic elements I'm afraid of losing. This list all boils down to the fear of losing my family, my reputation, my comfort, or my life.

The concept of fight-or-flight introduces the fact that we will each respond to fear in different physical ways. As we further unpack the idea of fear being a blocker of hope, we can dig a little deeper to see different ways in which our fear manifests in our emotions. Fear itself is not characterized as an emotion, but fear does stimulate many of them. Fear can trigger anger, panic, or sadness. It can also trigger doubt.

If we take the thought of fear appearing when there is the potential of something else disappearing, we have created an environment of doubt, which is the disbelief or uncertainty of something that is true. Doubt is the initial cause of hopelessness. If doubt is the disbelief that something is true and hopelessness is simply the lack of hope, then in the midst of a bomb-exploding life situation, if you doubt that there is any hope to be found, you find yourself immediately in a place of hopelessness. If this hopelessness does not become an arrow pointing you up, then the slide through the negative effects of hopelessness will begin. If we do not believe there can be hope, when we do not trust that what our hope is in will stay in our lives, disbelief breeds hopelessness, and we fear the result to follow.

However, we are intelligent creatures, created to have dominion over everything else that is on earth, so doubt doesn't always feel as if we are giving up, but can instead often feel quite logical.

Uttering the phrase *There is no hope* can come from a posture of distress and angst as we glance around feeling a severe lack of confidence in our current situation. But we are all different, and different personalities manifesting similar feelings often results in different takes on an emotion. For some, after contemplating whatever situation they are in and logically weighing out the *what is* with the *what it needs to be*, an obvious answer can be the calmly and rationally (at least to them) phrase, *Well, there's no hope.*

From either angle, from the anxiety-filled to the rationally thought out, a doubt in hope is still a disbelief in the power of God, a disbelief in His ability to bring hope to each and every situation we face and settling instead for a human-controlled version.

Each of us have been in a situation in which our plans are not working out like we thought. When this happens, the decision needs to be made to either cut our losses and move on to the next thing or realize that we are exactly where we are meant to be so we must learn to be content. Deciding between the two is on the top-ten toughest decisions list.

Facing adversity is a common course in life, just listen to any post-game interview in college football. I guarantee more than one coach or player will comment on the adversity they faced in whatever game they just won. When it comes to pushing that well-known boulder up a hill, the question is whether you are supposed to keep pushing it to the top where you will see the answer you have been seeking or whether to let the thing just roll back down so that your hands are free to take a different course.

The answer is not one that I can tell you, because with each situation there is a different set of circumstances that needs to be considered. There will be times to keep pushing, there will be times to let go, there will be times to follow the example of Ruth and be content to not push or let go, but to just sit and "glean from the field where you are planted," but never are those times to be decided when we are overpowered with the feeling of hopelessness. Even if the answer is not clear, one thing I can promise is that if your decision is based on doubting that there is another way, you are not resting in hope, you are letting the fear of doubt block your view.

Sometimes hope doesn't result in a clear answer written out with all the details. Most times hope is simply just hope—the enduring trust that your future is secure because of what Jesus did in the past, regardless of the clarity of your present view. Remember, God has promised us hope and a future. Rest in that promise.

Comparison is another element triggered by fear. As I look at my list of fears, there are more than a handful that produce the thought of what others will think of me. Comparison, my friend, as Teddy Roosevelt so wisely said, is the thief of joy. Not only can it rob you of relationship with others as you are tempted to hide your full self because you assume it does not measure up to someone else's gifts or another's standards, but it can also rob you of the thankfulness you can have for what God has done in your life. If you are busy looking at the talent of another, you miss seeing the beautiful ways God has gifted you.

Even more detrimental to your growth and knowledge of hope is comparison, the fear that you do not measure up, and it can also keep you from going to Him and growing in Him when you feel that your issue is not as significant as someone else's.

We have only had to make two visits to the ER so far in our parenting life, an amazing feat when you think of the she-nanigans three boys can get into. A busy ER is a scary but also fascinating place. Lives from diverse walks convene in the same building because of various injuries all under the category of emergency. No one wants to wait long, but then again no one wants to get first dibs either because that usually means you are far worse off than another. Educated people discern the situations at hand and put them in order, rushing some in, triaging others, and asking still others to wait for hours at times for their turn with a doctor.

When you attempt to compare your life with another, you are tempted to come to the conclusion that your struggle is not really that big of a deal. It is not as big a problem as _____ has. I'll just forget about it; I'll just handle it myself.

We are taught that one sin does not outweigh another in the eyes of God; he sees them all as just sin. Likewise, God does not love one of His children more than another. He does not give precedence to one of His children over another because their struggle seems to be harder, to go deeper. He is omnipresent. His hope does not run out and He is able to fill us all, heal us all, at the same time. Do not triage yourself, do not sit idly in the waiting room. God is bigger than that.

Yes, we must learn to put things in perspective. Yes, we must learn and grow from our past so that we can apply those lessons to our future, but your story is your story and the Author of our lives places us each in the scenarios needed to mold us into the beings whom He is calling us to be. No two pasts are the same, no two futures will be the same, and no future will look the way you've created it in your own mind. Always, however, always there is One who brings peace as you learn to embrace His promises for your life, and His truth will bring you comfort in whatever situation your find yourself.

Comparing yourself to another can also result in the fear that you are missing something. Have you ever found yourself in a similar situation as a friend, relative, or coworker, and noticed how easily they seem to be handling it while you yourself are losing your ever-loving mind? It can't just be me. Now seems to be a great time to reiterate that we are all different, YOU are wonderfully different, uniquely created with a personality unlike any other, and therefore with a unique way of responding to what appears in life.

If you find yourself thinking that you must be crazy, must be missing something and lacking answers to your problem, I can say in all honesty that yes, you are missing something, but no you are far from crazy. That process of sanctification we spoke of earlier is a lifelong one. With each new difficulty, bomb-exploding or not, we are confronted with the fact that we don't have it all together, we don't know how to fix it all, there are pieces to our puzzle that aren't here. So, yes, while we will always be gaining new pieces, we will always be missing plenty as well. Hope, however, is one thing that we do not have to miss.

We are imperfect people living in an imperfect world, but praise God that He is much more patient than we are, because as imperfect people we would have given up on ourselves long ago. He is ever faithful. He is watching, guiding, waiting, loving. He is not giving up. When you find yourself in the midst of a panic attack, emotional meltdown, spiritual dry spell, confusing situation, or just a standard rough day, when you find yourself wanting to get defensive or wanting to hide your head in the sand, you are missing hope. Comparison and fear are blocking your view of God seeing you exactly where you are and promising to be with you through it.

No one has it all together. The facades you are seeing are not real. The beautifully kept house on Instagram has piles of papers sitting just outside the shot. The mom with the perfectly coiffed kids just lost her temper in the parking lot. The marriage that looks like it came straight from a movie went through hell and back to discover what true love really looks like.

One sure way to see hope instead of letting fear block the way is to remember that you need it. Let hopelessness point you to your need to be boosted up and over the fence. If you put on your mask every morning, if you live pretending that all is well, you can't open yourself up to the hope that is vital in your life. In the words of singer/songwriter Jill Phillips, "Don't whitewash the truth about yourself, 'cause nobody's got it all together. If you want to be like everyone else well nobody's got it all together."[13]

Dare to be transparent. Dare to be vulnerable. Dare to admit out loud that you are stuck, that you are hurting, that you don't get it, that you don't have it all together.

It's easy, way too easy, to let fear take over and push hope out, but fear is not from God. He did not give us a Spirit of fear but of power and of love and of a sound mind. (2 Timothy 1:7) What we do have is hope, given through love, and His perfect love casts out those fears. (1 John 4:18) When those fears are out, it's Him that can come fully in. Admit your fears, list them out and see where they are blocking your view. And after that, ask God to enter into those places.

If you are already His, His Spirit is within you, ready and able to work. If you are not already His, if you have not yet admitted that you cannot do this on your own and submitted to the knowledge that only through Christ can you be whole, then I pray now that you will. Let Him fill the places that fear is currently taking up. Let Him work in you and with you and through you, filling you with the hope that overflows.

How Distractions Block Hope

Running in, out, and around our home are three awesome, crazy, beautiful blond-haired boys. Somehow in our thirteen years of parenting we have cultivated an environment of good communication, meaning we actually talk about things, things that we do not remember ever talking about with our parents. It's a blessing upon blessing to get to be the recipient of what is going on inside their little growing minds, even if, as boys, some of it is quite bizarre and occasionally disgusting.

However, no gifting is perfect, and as much as I love the desire they have to tell us all the things, the problem comes when they literally tell us ALL THE THINGS! My darling babies hop off the bus and into our car and immediately and simultaneously begin spewing everything they have either kept inside for the past seven school hours or everything they thought, said, and did for the past seven school hours, and I find myself trying to listen and respond to the most important and most random situations of the day while we all pile out of the car into the house and begin the process of unloading backpack and lunchbox paraphernalia.

I freely admit that there are days where it feels as if my body rebels and begins to shut down because it has heard enough words about enough things and just cannot take anymore. As my brain fills to max capacity and nothing else will fit in the space between my ears, I have subconsciously/consciously learned to just go about whatever I am doing, filling in with the correct timing of "Uh-huh," "Oh yeah?," "How fun," and "That stinks," not really in tune to the information that is being sent my way.

While I absolutely feel that this is a necessary mama tool that helps on those days when you need to hold on to the little sanity you have left, if left unchecked it becomes a huge problem.

In 2006, Adam Sandler starred in a movie called *Click* in which his character was a workaholic architect trying to climb the ladder of success at his firm. Exhausted by the toll work and family life can take, he stumbled across a crazy salesman played by Christopher Walken, an actor who always embodies the perfect amount of kookiness. Sandler's character is given a universal remote that allows him to fast-forward and rewind various parts of his life in order to skip them or hurriedly get them over with so that he has the opportunity to accomplish the work that will get him ahead in life. The only problem is that, though he feels as if the event is zipping by, for the rest of the family, time goes by like normal, and the only thing they see is a vacant face and absent father and husband for the majority of life. Thankfully, **spoiler alert**, he learns his lesson before it's too late, and the magic remote propels him back in time, giving him the chance to relive his life in a whole-heartedly present way.

Those little boys who fill my heart will always have words, and they are going to keep them coming, praise Jesus, because I already miss the baby voices they used to use as the stories that now come my way are shared with the maturing voices of youth. By *clicking on* too often that sanity-saving device my mind has developed instead of saving it for emergency situations, I miss funny and vital information about their lives. I miss needed parenting moments that only come through reading between the lines of their stories. When I allow blocking out to become a daily part of living, I begin to be permanently distracted from my job as a parent and miss what is waiting right in front of me. And I don't want to miss a moment, because those boys are some of my favorite things to see.

Just as fear can keep us from looking up and asking to be carried to a better view of hope, distractions can cloud our judgment and cover up the necessary clues required to help us notice our need for hope. Distractions block our way to hope by causing our eyes to shift away from where hope is found.

Distractions are everywhere, E.V.E.R.Y.W.H.E.R.E. Our homes are a minefield of items that can take our attention away at any given moment. Stepping outside our homes into the world provides so many distractions that it hurts my head to even try to name them all. There are even men and women whose sole job is to create and market products that grab your attention and sway your thoughts.

I have lost count of the number of hours that have flitted away in my life because I was just going to check social media real quick, only to get wrapped up in something meaningless, then look up to see that an hour has gone by.

Going back to that trip to Vegas (you know the one where it took me three days to notice a curtain posing as the side of a building), well, it was there where it hit me that the main reason places like Vegas are built is to assist you in forgetting about your reality. *What happens in Vegas stays in Vegas* because it wouldn't be possible anywhere else. On a similar note, while we have yet to make the pilgrimage to visit the Happiest Place on Earth, I can imagine it produces the same effects, just in a slightly more family appropriate atmosphere.

I am not going to lead a revolt to rid our world of all electronic devices in favor of embracing a more Amish-like existence. I am also not saying advertisers are terrible people who just want to brainwash you or that Disney World is of the devil because they are trying to convince you that, in comparison, you live a dull and unhappy life. Good can come from anywhere and be in anything on this earth because what God created is good and He can use it all for good. I am, however, trying to make sure you know that anything, and I mean anything, also carries the potential to take your attention away from where it needs to be.

All of this is to say that believe me, I know, I understand, I am with you. As I walk you through a few things that can turn your eyes away from the true hope in Christ, I'm really just giving you a glimpse of the things that turn my eyes away and praying fervently that maybe there is someone out there that needs to hear it, too.

I am a Type-A; list-making; stay-busy-so-I-don't-have-to-think-about-it; hide-from-reality-in-books, -movies, and -tasks; good at faking; keep the peace; stuff-it-until-it-goes-away queen of distractibility. I would literally sit and listen to a friend share their struggles for hours and encourage them to talk about it and pray about it and share it with whomever it needed to be shared, and then even share with them my own thoughts and struggles and so on. But in my own life, when it comes down to it, I will distract myself temporarily with almost anything and cling to the quick peace it brings and not to the unfailing hope that I was adopted as a child of the King.

We all have those things we immediately seek to provide a distraction, things that we think will make everything better in just a moment. Those distractions are tempting because of that very reason—they are immediate. But just like that candy craving that produces a brief energetic sugar high when consumed, a crash follows almost immediately after, leaving you more lethargic than you were before. Just like that list of fears that came so easily to my mind, the list of well-used distractions comes just as quickly. Can you think of any for yourself?

I'll admit, in my own life I knew from the beginning that everything was going to eventually be okay. I knew that months or years down the road this experience will have made us stronger, but I also admit that I wanted to do everything in my power to distract me from the junk I'd have to go through before I reached that point. I wanted to just get to the end without mucking through the middle. In Romans 8 it says, "Consider the sufferings of your present time are not worth comparing with the glory that will be revealed in us." (CSB) I believed the end result of that promise to be true, but I did not want to have to go through the middle to get there.

In the midst of recovering from a bomb of reality that sends you reeling down the slide of hopelessness, there are days when you will struggle mightily, internally and externally, with facing what is going on in your life. In those moments, it's very difficult to believe that verse from Romans 8 because it feels like a promise too far off in the distance to be true. These are the days when all you want to do is race with all your might to the finish line and get the lessons over with, or all you want to do is disappear and pretend it never happened.

That desperate need to distract ourselves from reality connects directly to our fear manifested in doubt. We simply do not believe there is something better. Friend, check your heart. Are you numbing yourself with distractions? Like me, of course you are; so what distractions are you numbing yourself with?

While we do our best to block our own view with anything that will bring immediate comfort or temporary amnesia, God will not let us hide for long. He sees you all the time, whether you are looking up for Him or not. His desire for you is not to numb the pain but to replace it with His goodness, the goodness of hope that will never fail, that will anchor you steadfastly to Him so that even though you might go through a storm, the chain will never break and leave you adrift. This experience is the realization of the promise that suffering can never compare to what will be. A life anchored in hope can not only weather all things, but, like Forrest and Lieutenant Dan's lone shrimping boat in *Forrest Gump*, such a life can come out of the storm revealing glory for the one who held it together.

The Spirit, when He lifts you up over the fence to get the real view, is enabling you to do what we are commanded in Colossians 3:2 to do: "Set your mind on things above and not on earthly things." (ESV) Earthly things might feel satisfying for a short time, but they will never fill you up enough so that you never have to go back for another hit. Those things we are looking at, those squirrels that send our eyes suddenly sideways, are the things we can see easily, but "we must look not at the things which are seen, but are not seen; for the things which are seen are temporary, but the things which are unseen are eternal." (2 Corinthians 3:18, ESV)

Those things I use to pull my attention away and hide me from reality also tear me away from my Father and the hope He gives. Hiding in a fantasy-world bubble of self-produced perfection that can burst at any moment can never compare to living a real, imperfect life with a hope that never fails.

How Idols Block Hope

It was September 12, the day after the entire story had finally been revealed, and we were sitting in our living room, on those same couches, but side by side this time as our friend and pastor sat across from us. The purpose of his visit was three-fold. The first was because he loved us both and wanted to make sure we felt the presence of loving friends. The second was to have a *How are you right this second?* check-in because in the aftermath of bomb-like situations, emotions can change in an instant. The third was to tell me one important thing: *This was not my fault.* Sure, no person is perfect, no marriage is perfect, but there was nothing I could have done or could have said to stop it, and there was nothing I did or did not do to cause it. Those decisions and choices were made by two people, and I was not one of them.

For a guilt-struggling, second-guessing girl like myself, these were refreshing words to hear. This man who God used to breathe the Gospel into my life more than anyone else to date, went on to share that if I learned anything in the aftermath of forgiveness and healing it would be just an added bonus to what God was already doing and going to do in the heart of my husband.

These words did not give me an excuse to sit on the sidelines with a pompous *See, I told you I wasn't the problem* attitude. These words became an invitation to think about myself without the stress of feeling like there was a specific failure I needed to fix or an obvious fault that was on display. N.T. Wright said, "Often that's all it takes, someone you trust says one or two sentences, and a door opens into a whole new world."[14] A door was opened for me that day. It opened to a desire to search myself, to reach for that extra growth that could come through changes in my heart as well.

That moment, those words shared directly from a heart of love to a heart needing to be loved, marked the beginning point of not only a restored marriage—which is a wonderful, blessed thing—but also more importantly, a fully restored me, a me that knows better the promises of God and knows what having them hold on to you feels like, no matter what seems to fall apart next.

When you watch the man you love walk the road of Psalm 51, when you see him struggle under the guilt of his actions and the pain of mining his heart and going through the refiner's fire in order to find the pure metals underneath, sitting on the sidelines is an option you can choose, free from judgment. But in the end, it wasn't the one I wanted to take. Walking that road with him, mining my own heart alongside him and walking through the fire myself was the only place I could be, because I needed it too.

No matter what scenario has brought about your life explosion, whether it's within a relationship where the other party wants nothing to do with reconciliation, an event in which you are the only one involved, or the million that can fit in between, even if you know you are in no way at fault, I urge you to walk the road of mining your own heart and finding what you may have put up as a roadblock in front of you, because growing in the Lord will never produce negative results.

When you become a believer, you surrender your life to God, admitting that though you may try, you just cannot make things right and good. In that moment of humbling beauty you are essentially asking God to do what it says in Psalm 51:10.

You want Him to create a pure heart within you. The only way to make that possible is to let Him first clean out the stuff that's already there.

There are many things I love to do with my time. Two that take up the most of those precious extra moments that are not already occupied by work and family are gardening and refinishing furniture. Both of these hobbies require a large amount of cleaning out before putting in.

To boost the curb appeal of your home, one cannot just dig a hole and shove in something green and leafy. First, you must remove what is in the way. Whether it's the grass that's been living there for years because you envision a new garden bed in that spot, the weeds that have taken over the area where beautiful things are supposed to be growing, or the not-quite-your-taste (read: ugly) bushes the well-meaning previous owners thought looked just fine, a cleaning out of sorts must be done so that there is room for the new.

The same is true for refinishing furniture. Slapping some paint on a piece that has been buried in an attic somewhere is going to accomplish nothing but getting dust and cobwebs all mixed up in your paint brush. You must take the time to dust it off, wipe it down, and prepare the surface so that what you want to put on, what you want to add to it, will really stick and not just flake off a few weeks down the road.

The things we put in front of our relationship with God, the things we purposely hold up in front of our eyes to stare at, block us from seeing Him and the hope He will provide, the hope He is currently providing. These idols in our lives become the self-constructed fence ruining the view.

It took me many years of Christian life to realize that when God says not to put any other gods before him, He was not just referring to golden calves and little pagan figurines prevalent in tents during biblical times. He was talking about anything, ANYTHING, that I place at the top of my list of priorities, anything above the number one spot where He should reside.

"Idolatry," according to Scott Hafemann in his book *The God of Promise and the Life of Faith*, "is the practice of seeking the source and provision of what we need either physically or emotionally in someone or something other than the one true God. It is the tragically pathetic attempt to squeeze the life out of lifeless forms that cannot help us meet our real needs."[15]

One Sunday morning while serving as the children's church teacher in the seven- and eight-year-old class, we were discussing the story of Elijah having a "prophet-off" (or whatever the best term is to use when describing a dance-off between prophets of a god) with a group of men hired by King Ahab to be prophets of Baal. In this story in 1 Kings 18, Elijah is trying to prove that the god Baal they are praying to is not real, so he asks them to build an altar and set an offering on top of it but not to light it on fire. Instead, he asks the prophets to call upon their god, Baal, to start the fire. To illustrate the point, I took my turquoise water bottle and set it in the middle of our table and said, "Okay kids, here's Baal, now do you want to ask him to start a fire?" They giggled and joked and gave the desired response this teacher was hoping for: of course, that water bottle can't do anything on its own. And neither can any other idols we create for ourselves.

We will all put our trust in something, place something at the top to hold on to when life becomes too much. If that thing at the top is not God, then hope will never be the result. You cannot ask something to produce what only God can give, no matter how much you may want to. Whether that idol is yourself, another person, your occupation, money, the spotlight, or a substance, it will not and cannot fulfill. Blaise Pascal, a 1600's mathematician and philosopher is often quoted as saying, "There is a God-shaped vacuum in the heart of every person which cannot be filled by any created thing, but only by God, the Creator." Things of the earth cannot fill a void shaped by God no matter which way we turn them and how hard we try to shove them in.

In Jonah 2:8 we learn that those who cling to worthless idols turn away from God's love for them. Ezekiel 14 has the Lord describing idols as wicked stumbling blocks set up before them. Even the most innocent of things put before God can produce wicked returns.

Some of the idols in your life are obviously damaging and you may already notice their negative influence in your life. However, many of the idols in our lives might not look like bad things in our eyes. Your kids are adorable most of the time, but if they drive every decision you make, they have become idols. Your husband might be a hot and awesome fella, but if your desire to please him goes above your desire to please God, he's an idol. The ministry work you do at church or another part of the worldwide Kingdom is wonderful and helpful to many, but if it feeds your pride and is what your identity is based on, it's most definitely an idol. Work, money, exercise, ministries, volunteering, crafting, sports, video games, and anything else you spend your time doing are not bad things, but it only takes a little twist to turn them from good things to enhance your enjoyment of the life God gives us on Earth to idols that suck that life right out of you.

Paul Tripp, or P. Diddy T as we refer to him in our house, wrote, "Could it be that that desire for a good thing has become a bad thing because that desire has become a ruling thing?"[16] Think about those things that have become such a ruling thing in your life that they are blocking the view to see the hope that is intended to rule your heart.

When your eyes are on everything else, when your mind is captivated by what the world brings you and is not focused on God, then it is impossible to see hope. Hope comes from a life with Christ. In a life that puts everything else in front of Him, hope cannot reign. It's not just enough to pluck out the idols and cast them away; the most important step is replacing them with a satisfying hope that will always fill your need. If I pull every weed from my garden and do nothing to prevent their return, it won't be long until they are all back, blocking the way. Something must fill that spot and take root so that nothing else can. The same is true in our hearts. For hope to remain in us, we must remain in Him.

5

Abiding

I had no idea the brain could take in so much information at once. I spent years and years in school striving to be a straight-A student, studying and memorizing and staring at notes until I could visualize them in my mind for when they were not in front of me, but nothing prepared me for this. No amount of cramming prepared my system for the sheer amount of information I am having to take in and process and file away in its appropriate categories.

Sitting and staring, my mind is reeling.

Sitting and staring, my heart is racing.

Sitting and staring, my brain has no ability to tell the rest of my body what to do because it is so occupied with the task at hand, downloading every single ounce of information that in any way pertains to the situation that has been revealed.

Thank God someone told me that in the long run it won't hurt my kids to eat frozen chicken nuggets and binge-watch Curious George *for a while, because that stupid man in a yellow hat who leaves a monkey alone ALL THE FREAKING TIME no matter how much trouble he got into the last time is in many ways a better parent that I can be right now.*

Praying, pleading. All I can think is I need to take it all in. *As hard as it is, I need to take it all in, now. I do not want to be surprised later with new information. I do not want to ignore something now that rears its ugly head weeks or months down the road and that will require going back to ground zero. I do not want to hide, I do not want to ignore it, so the only option is to stand up and walk straight into the fire. Make me feel the heat if you have to, drag me down to the bottom if you have to, make me sit in the muck if you have to, but just do not leave me down there alone. I cannot handle it alone.*

I am in a current season of sleep where I am constantly fighting with my pillow. Years ago my husband and I dropped what felt like a fortune to our newlywed selves on some really good down pillows. The problem is, that was fourteen years ago and those geese have been squashed to death by now, one pillow in particular. Now, on a nightly basis, we find ourselves complaining about this one, flat, used-to-be-fluffy, pillow, switching out the good one with each other every few nights so as to not be completely selfish, and folding this flat thing eighty-seven times to try and make it keep our heads from falling straight to the mattress below. This is all instead of making the time to buy new ones, because I am also in a season of life where the only places we have time to go are Target and the grocery store, and while there is many a thing I will load into my Amazon cart and have delivered in two days, a pillow isn't one of them. I need to be able to feel it and squish it and punch it into submission in person to make sure it can fulfill the maximum amount of comfort that I desire. I like comfort.

A friend's son has always called comfortable *cozy*. "I want to wear my cozy pants" is a phrase he would use every morning to remind her of his desired outfit as she got him dressed. "But this isn't cozy" is another phrase often uttered when her choice did not fit his basic requirement.

Adults are essentially large kids when it comes to being *cozy* or seeking comfort. Our daily lives can often be a stream of making decisions based on what will give us the most comfort in any given situation. Our choice of clothing is made to make sure we feel comfortable in the temperatures we will be spending our day in. The jobs we sought out are the ones that we felt most comfortable achieving. Our food choices are made to bring comfort to not only our bodies but our taste buds as well. The extracurricular activities we choose comfort our minds and highlight our talents, making us feel better emotionally than we would without being involved in them.

Then, at the end of the day, when we have made it back to the home that we spend time and money on to make as comfortable for us as possible, we base the success of our day on how much comfort the day held and how much discomfort it lacked. If comfort outweighed discomfort we deem it a good day; if discomfort outweighed the comfort, our impression is the opposite. Even if some of the choices made are ones that have to stretch us to uncomfortable levels, we live for the day, either at the end of a week or the end of a big project, where we can cuddle in the comforts of our choice in order to melt away whatever discomfort we have not been able to avoid for that time period.

You ready for this? When we live a life where every decision is based upon personal comfort, we are living a life of selfishness. Yes, being called selfish stinks, and it is a tough pill to swallow, especially for this girl who thought her life was full of love and compassion for others. But the more I started digging into my own heart the more I realized that even if the choices I make happen to benefit others as well, when my decisions are made through comfort-seeking glasses my only option is selfishness; my choices will be for me and me alone, no matter how much I may believe I am reaching out to others and putting their needs first.

A former pastor once mentioned that God was not interested in our comfort. It irritated some people. It irritated me. But in the end, I get it. His point was that God takes you where He wants you to go, where you need to go, to produce in you the character you need to fulfill His will, to fulfill the calling He has on your life. We cannot be brought through new challenges and learn new things by only choosing the comfort of what we already know.

We like comfortable, we love being cozy. However, it can also be truly detrimental to our hearts. If we are comfortable, we forget things. We forget we need a Savior, because what is there to be saved from in the midst of comfort? We forget we need the Spirit, because why do I need guidance when I'm all cozy and comfy? We forget we need a Heavenly Father, because why do I need love from another when I'm feeling so good wrapped up under my blanket of me-ness? We forget that we have been called to serve others, because who wants to get up from their warm and comfortable spot of what and whom we know to enter an uncomfortable world full of others' needs?

To God, it is getting to our hearts and our souls that matters most.

If you are already a Christian, one of your first reactions to this might be to think that, of course, you know that already; of course, you know you need the Trinity (a.k.a. Father, Son, and

Holy Spirit); everyone knows that. You may know that in your head, but do you really believe it in your heart? Deep down, in the innermost places of your being, do you really believe that what you believe is really real?[17] Do you go about your day to day seeing it in action, saying it with your words and feeling it at the root of every situation? The answer, of course, is no. Why? Because we're broken. Because we try to fix our lives and ourselves with other things. Because we get comfortable.

If you are not a believer already, your reaction might be to turn tail and run so that you can hang on to the comfortable life you have already created on your own before someone tells you that you might have to let it go. Please don't! Just wait and listen, because I am not going to tell you that the answer to the dilemma of selfish comfort-seeking choices is to purposely throw yourself into terrible, uncomfortable situations. What I want you to know is that comfort CAN still reign, it DOES still exist, EVEN in the most uncomfortable of experiences.

It took a bit of searching and pondering to determine that, and while my pastor had a valid point, God led me to understand a slightly different one. God is not disinterested in our comfort; I one hundred percent believe that He IS interested in our comfort. God wants us to feel secure in every situation, He desires for our hearts, in their innermost parts, to be completely warm and cozy. He just wants those feelings to come from the right place, to emanate from the correct source: Him. Comfort, like grace, like mercy, like hope, is a gift.

When we seek out comforts on our own, we will inevitably, eventually find ourselves in a place of discomfort, because the comfort we create cannot last. Think for a moment and remember something you did, bought, or created to give you a sense of comfort. For me, a seemingly innocent one is Dr.

Pepper. This deliciousness, preferably in a frosted can, has put many a smile on my face. But the feelings of calm those sips brought never lasted; instead, they conditioned my mind and body over the years to crave one in times of stress, or sadness, or frustration, because it is one thing I repeatedly sought out to soothe and relax me on a crazy day. Naptime Dr. Pepper was a legitimate event when my boys were small, and even after years of understanding that lasting comfort comes from true hope, I can still feel my body yearn for that taste any time any of those mentioned emotions rise up within me.

But not every comfort I seek out is as trivial as a simple carbonated beverage and neither is the retail therapy, cleaning binges, workouts, or whatever else you innocently seek out to set yourself at ease. Because like that icy, smile-inducing liquid, eventually the feeling of discomfort will return, and there is only so much you can buy, clean, or sweat out before you must up the ante. When we begin seeking comforts on our own, they will slowly stop fulfilling their intended purpose as much as they once did and when this happens it causes us to reevaluate our choices and make changes that will bring the comfort back again. Some of those reevaluated choices drag us down into deeper, more serious things.

Addictions do not happen in an instant. They happen over time, one step deepening into another as comfort that could never really fill was sought; with discomfort returning over and over, forcing the need to see if there are any other substances, places, or experiences that will give what we desire.

I have no authority to aid someone who has drifted into the land of serious, potentially life-destroying addiction, but I do know that none of us are as immune to it as we think we are and "but for the Grace of God there go I." Nothing in life apart from God is secure. Comfort is real and available through the hope of Jesus, and without Him a lifelong battle of cause-and-effect choices will forever ensue to keep us firmly stationed in that sweet spot of self-made comfort instead of the real Comfort that never wears off. We just need to understand what comfort is meant to look and feel like and not what we have imagined it is supposed to do.

As we discussed in Chapter 2, much like the way the word *hope* has been distorted over generations, the word *comfort* has been treated similarly. Comfort, in our minds, is a state of personal perfection where all things are exactly how we would like them to be so that there is no stress, just peace. Peace, which we will talk about later in the book, like comfort, does not come from perfection. Each of these scenarios that our hearts long for come from hope, come from knowing the promises we have through Jesus and trusting in them.

God is completely concerned with our comfort because He knows He is the only one who can provide true comfort to us, the comfort found in the person and work of Christ for us. He loves us too much to let us go on believing that the answer to all our discomfort is a beverage. Because of that, because He is such a loving God, He allows us to be uncomfortable for one and only one reason: to seek Him. To sit in His lap. To cry out His name. To lay all our burdens down at that cross and not pick them up again. To remember what He has done before and believe that He will do it again and thank Him for all of it. He does this because He knows there is no other way, there is no other true source.

Andrew Peterson, singer/songwriter and author, wrote a brilliant children's book series called *The Wingfeather Saga*, in which the main character is a boy named Janner.[18] Andrew shared that because he created Janner and knew whom he needed Janner to be at the end of the last book, it was his job as the author to take this boy through all the situations he would need to go through to mold him into the person he would need to be with all the wisdom and character qualities he would need to become who he was intended to be in the end. What a beautiful, earthly representation of what our Divine Creator does for us.

"For we are God's masterpiece," Ephesians 2:10 says. "He has created us anew in Christ Jesus so we can do the good things he planned for us long ago." (NLT)

Though in life there have been, and will be again, different bombs that leave me with no other option but to completely cling to hope, through that single experience and the massive amount of ripples that came with it, life is now much different than what I imagined for myself. In many ways, however, it is beautifully and mercifully similar, because in my midst is a loving Heavenly Father, a husband, children, and specific friends that are still here, next to each other, bearing burdens, living life as children of the King, better and closer and able to tell an even greater story of His Goodness.

"Praise be to the God and Father of our Lord Jesus Christ, the Father of compassion and the God of all comfort, who comforts us in all our troubles, so that we can comfort those in any trouble with the comfort we ourselves receive from God. For us as we share abundantly in the sufferings of Christ, so also our comfort abounds through Christ. If we are distressed, it is for your comfort and salvation; if we are comforted, it is for your comfort, which produces in you patient endurance of the same sufferings we suffer. And our hope for you is firm, because we know that just as you share in our sufferings, so also you share in our comfort."—1 Corinthians 1:3–7 (NIV)

He is making us new. He is renewing a right spirit within us. He is making us holy. He is renewing us day by day. Comfort is found even in the most uncomfortable messes because of Jesus, and the masterpieces we become will bring comfort to others through the good He has planned for us to do. To do all these things requires situations that do not allow us to hide in the world we have built for ourselves. The houses we build on shaky ground to try to give ourselves the feelings of security will fall, and out of love for us God will blow up the pitiful world we attempted to create alone so that we will see the better one He has built, the world we cannot live without.

Are you convinced that God cares deeply for your comfort? My heart desires that you know and understand how completely true that is. When you see and comprehend His love for you through His desire to bring you comfort, true comfort, you are able to fully believe He cares for you, and if He cares for you, then the promises He has made to you are to be trusted. If you trust in His promise then you can hold onto hope, because the presence of hope is one of those dear promises made and fulfilled in the coming of His Son.

When one truth is discovered it leads to another and another and another. If this, then this. As these truths stack up in our understanding, our eyes are opened to a picture that is being revealed, not so much of our own life, but of the One who created our life. It is all encompassing, all connecting, all a giant pretzel of stories weaving in and out of each other, though, if untwisted, still resulting in one straight line, one path twirled into a beautifully intricate pattern.

There is a key to this concept though, a key we have a part in holding, putting into the lock and turning so that the click is heard and the knob can be turned. True comfort is an ever-present thing that we cannot produce or fulfill with the items and experiences we seek out. Comfort comes from merely abiding in the Son He so lovingly gave to the world. The Son whose very essence is the hope we so need. The key is to abide.

In the months that followed my husband's affair, I was doing an intense amount of reading and studying and journaling. At some point John 15 entered the *to-study* list. While reading, one word kept jumping out at me until I finally stopped to look up its meaning. It's amazing how many shift changes your mind and heart can have in a split second, when before that you had felt stuck for what seemed like forever. It makes me think back to a giant maze my friends and I would visit at the beach when we were younger. We'd spend endless moments deciding which way to turn at some points, while at others we'd quickly blaze around corners, finding our way more and more with each directional shift. That day, that moment when one word stuck out among so many others, a shift began, another turn on the making me *me* trail, in how I look at my relationship with Christ.

Honestly, it's probably not new to most people, but it was a lightbulb moment for me. In a conversation with a friend, she shared that she felt as if her lightbulb moments aren't really impressive or anything earth shattering to most people. I assured her that she was not the only one who felt that. A lie we believe, a lie that keeps us from following the commands written all through Psalms and other places in Scripture to proclaim what He has done, is the fear that we are not sharing anything new or impressive, that the lessons we learn are less than extraordinary and maybe not even as exciting as plain ordinary. Yes, God has performed extraordinary things in history that immediately caught the gaze of not only His people but of others looking on; but His greatest gift, His most extraordinary feat, came to the humble setting of a stable in a little town, to ordinary people like you and me.

Elijah, it tells us in the book of 1 Kings, did not see the presence of God in a mighty and fierce wind, or in an earth-shattering quake, or in a hot fire with the ability to produce smoke seen for miles and miles. Elijah knew the presence of God was there because of a soft whisper. Psalm 119:130 says "the unfolding of Your words gives light; it gives understanding to the simple." (ESV)

Your lightbulb moment, whatever it is, still shines light, and in the darkness a little light is all someone needs to begin to see. So, let's get back to this one that God switched on for me.

Looking at John 15, you might recollect the vine and branches and all the gardening that is going on. In previous readings, I had thought more about what is being taken away, just as it says in the first three verses. He cuts off what is in me that doesn't bear fruit. He prunes what does bear fruit so that it will bear more fruit. Painful at times, but makes sense: out with the bad, in with the good, and then make the good even better. But then that word that caught my heart's attention comes for the first time, "Abide in me because you cannot bear fruit by yourself." And then again, "Abide in me and I in you and you will bear much fruit." And again, "Abide in me and in my words and what you ask will be done." And again, "Abide in my love." (ESV paraphrasing)

All of a sudden, instead of focusing on what God was taking away, my eyes instead focused on where He wanted me to be. His aim, as it turned out, was closeness.

I found two definitions when the sheer emotion felt from reading the word *abide* over and over sent me on a search. The first is that abiding is "to accept or act in accordance with a rule, decision, or recommendation."[19] As in, *You must abide by.*

When we are given a Savior who, as Hebrews 5:15 says, "is a high priest who is able to empathize with our weaknesses, because in every respect has been tempted as we are, yet without sin," (ESV) then we can be convinced that there is not another person we should accept or act in accordance with above Christ. Jesus understands you. That verse tells us that he empathizes with our weaknesses, each of our weaknesses, personally. Last time I looked, my plate was just as full as everyone else's, but it held very different things. My sufferings exist like everyone else's, but they are not all the same. My weaknesses are my weaknesses. He understands mine, He understands yours, He understands them all.

The list of synonyms went on to include *obey, observe, follow, hold to, conform to, stick to, stand by, uphold, accept, respect, defer to . . .* Can you imagine how much different your actions and decisions would be if looking to Christ, and what He said and did because He knows and understands us so well, was the first thing you did before anything else? That knowledge comes from abiding in Him, knowing Him, being one with Him, realizing that He is not just in us but also we are in Him. He is our covering. He is the face God sees when He looks at us.

The second definition for *abide* is "a feeling or memory that continues without fading or being lost."[20] It continues, remains, persists, stays. It survives.

When you are going through a period where nothing seems as it is supposed to be, when you are praying to rejoice, hope, love, and be satisfied in the Lord alone, but have no idea how to truly do it, abiding is the answer to it all. Christ will always continue without fading or being lost. He will remain. He survived. He lasts, persists, and stays. He is all of those things that

I want and need and all I have to do is stay with Him, to keep my branch connected to the vine that gives me life and produces in me fruit that the world needs.

Abide is a balm to the soul, a word that can be whispered to yourself in a moment, that sends the mind directly where it should go, toward the One in whom we need to abide. It needs to become a pathway to walk down over and over again until it is so well-worn that no thought of where to go is needed because habit has set in, and it is an involuntary action of life's journey to simply rest in Jesus.

I am so thankful for a Savior who asks me to abide in Him totally and completely so that I feel wanted and protected, guided and held fast. So that I feel the comfort we all so desire. Yes, abiding in Christ, in His love, sacrifice, plan, purpose, perfection, and life is the key, and as soon as we are His we can begin to feel His presence, to feel a difference, a lightness in our lives and hearts. But as much as we love instant solutions, understanding the answers can come much quicker sometimes than the installment of them into our lives.

Christ never leaves us, but we can often venture from Him. At first we may tiptoe out from under His wing for a quick peek and then run back. Next, it's out again a little further from the nest until our feet seem secure enough that we venture out so far that we stop looking to Him and begin looking at ourselves again instead. How do we learn to just stay?

When you are a child, you are warned against talking to strangers, and for good reason. Your parents love you and want to keep you safe. They know you are not capable of protecting yourself against bad things that could happen, and that you have not yet developed the capabilities to discern the people and environments around you. They give you rules to follow, tools to use, and lists of safe people to ask for help until you begin to grow up and are better able to navigate the world.

As you grow in age, you grow in relationship. I grew up in a small town, and the friends I made in early elementary school were the friends I still had when I graduated high school. New ones were added as people moved to town, and some were lost as people moved away. The natural process of growing apart took place with some as different interests were developed and teenage romance entered the picture, but for the most part I spent anywhere from ten to eighteen years with a group of people I knew well.

Then college came, and with it came moving away from home for the first time. Four short years later came marriage and another big move to a new place. In both of those transitions there was a blank slate for relationships. The people I met were new, therefore the process of gaining and giving trust started over. While I do believe that God has called me and you to be transparent with our stories for our own good and His glory, we are also warned to not give dogs what is sacred; so you have to foster relationships before they are completely formed.

You have to develop a relationship before you can open yourself to it. You have to feel safe before you give of yourself and your innermost thoughts. Yes, it can take time and patience, but more than anything else, it takes presence. It takes being with that person to grow in relationship. You can't grow without contact, without sharing space, even if that space is on a computer or phone screen at a distance of thousands of miles and multiple time zones. Without a connection to each other, the relationship is over before it begins.

The same is true for our relationship with God, with His Son, and with the Spirit left with us on this earth. The act of abiding is that connection; it's the way the relationship grows. It's how we get to know Him more fully and trust Him more securely.

Abiding in our Savior, resting in the shadow of His wings, means a direct, close-contact relationship with Him. Our sinful flesh will try to fight against that resting place, will try to drive a wedge between us or try to persuade us that stepping out on our own is not disobedience like we think, but encouraged independence that proves growth and maturity. I'll wager, we have each ventured out on our own, depending solely on ourselves and our abilities, only to end up seeing we need someone to lean on. There is no better place than with Jesus, and He wants us to lean on Him.

I am so thankful for that direct line, thankful there is a Father in heaven who knows me completely and has given me His Son to rest in to aid me in knowing Him better. The key is always His Son, abiding with Him is the secret to clinging to hope because abiding in Him brings about something else that makes clinging to hope even easier. Abiding in Him brings peace.

I love stories in the Bible that show us the humanity of the ones Jesus chose to follow him. Never once, except in Christ Himself, do we see a perfect person who has it all together and always makes the right decisions; it is indeed quite the opposite. Jesus had no option but to surround Himself with sinners because they were the only people who walked on earth with Him; but He made sure to surround himself with people who knew that they were sinners, who knew they were lost and needed finding.

Peter (Oh, how I love the gumption of Peter), who in one minute thinks he has it all together and in the next falls flat on his face, is a great example. He sees his Teacher walking toward him on the water, so he steps out of the boat, eyes trained on Jesus, and walks on the water himself. But the moment his eyes shift toward the wind around him and the sea beneath him, he sinks. His eyes were no longer stayed on the One who could save but on the elements that could destroy. I am so like Peter.

On the side of my right foot, much to my mother's dismay, is a tattoo, a birthday present to myself that fulfilled a decades-long desire. That tattoo, in delicate script, reads *Isaiah 26:3*. The verse it references says, "You keep him in perfect peace whose mind is stayed on you, because he trusts in you." (ESV) Perfect peace from nothing more than a mind stayed on Christ. Abiding is just looking at Jesus, and keeping me at peace is the result.

So, why tattoo that on my body, why put that in a place in a way that can never be erased? Because I have lost that peace more times than I would care to count; like Peter, I get out of the boat, but once I am there my eyes begin to stray. There I am, sitting with a mind full of peace, calm, and contentment, and suddenly it turns into a state of anxiety, emotional chaos, and irrational thought. The reason may vary, the environment may change, and the intensity may wave, but the core remains the same. An event, a situation, or a response allows my flesh to attempt to push out the Spirit and take my heart captive, making its home there instead. Since we are told in Scripture that out of the heart the mouth speaks, having a heart driven by our sin instead of by the Spirit will result in a whole other slew of issues.

Peace, like so many other words we have covered thus far, has a meaning that has changed over time as well. It is not a lack of stress, a lack of chaos; it is not based on circumstances. We can't claim only to feel at peace when life is going our way, but we also do not have to wait to feel peace until life is going our way. We might have the ability to foster around us a more comfortable and less chaotic life; we might see the good in granting ourselves margin and knowing our personalities well enough to see our own limits. While both are mature and healthy ways to live, they will not bring eternal peace, because we are not supposed to be able to create peace on our own.

Peace, that blessed feeling that sends hearts back to normal rhythms and breathing back to a purely involuntary action, is gifted to us through Christ, bringing harmony, which means *to be complete, to be whole*. Galatians 5:22 then gives us a third benefit of this fruit of the Spirit; peace, when truly felt, provides your heart with such overwhelming comfort, stopping you in your tracks because you can tangibly feel it overpowering all your humanity and placing in you instead a feeling of awe from the warmth enveloping your soul, filling all your empty places. Wholeness.

Peace cannot be explained through circumstance because peace can be felt regardless of the circumstance. Philippians 4 describes it as the peace that passes all understanding that guides our hearts and stays our minds in Christ because we are in communion with Him and our Father. That peace comes because of the presence in relationship. It comes because of communication, through getting to know Him better and trusting Him with our hearts. Peace comes from abiding, which is where it starts and where it ends, even if it takes many twists and turns to teach you how to remain there.

Those distinct moments in life where you have literally felt the wave of peace that passes all understanding are worth writing down and remembering, because when you feel the urge to head out alone or find that you already went out and don't know how to get back, it's those memories that hold reminders of the faithfulness of a good God who loves well and brings hope.

We love comfort. God grants us comfort through abiding in His Son. That abiding brings peace to our hearts and when peace reigns in our hearts, our eyes will see the hope all around.

6

Faith First

"What am I missing?"

The words came out of my mouth in sobs on the phone to my pastor and counselor as I paced up and down the small strip of carpet in the master bedroom of our rental home. It was one of those days, one where it all felt heavy on me again, not because I was learning too much, but because I did not think I was learning enough. Three of the four people involved in our situation had gone through life-altering, doubting-who-God-is-and-coming-back-to-Him experiences. Everyone, except me.

Why hadn't I hit rock bottom like everyone else, and is there something wrong with me that I haven't hit it? Do I even have a rock bottom to hit? Am I still on my way down? I desperately wanted MY lesson in the whole experience, the one God meant for me and only me. Yes, He was teaching me about marriage and allowing me to see Him work in the heart and life of my husband, but just as I felt like I was on the outside before, I still feel a bit on the outside now. I never doubted where God was. I felt His presence and His peace from day one, but dang it, just because I'm not the squeaky wheel doesn't mean I wouldn't like some grease every now and again.

"Sarah," came his voice over the phone while he proceeded to explain something to me about myself I had never seen, "are you giving God the chance to reveal something new to you or are you just trying to figure it all out yourself?"

In the most loving and gentle way possible, it was revealed to me exactly what my lesson was: to have faith in God's righteousness and not my own. From day one I felt God's peace and presence. I saw His hand in my past and how He had guided me through different situations and to different Scriptures and studies so that in the moment I needed them the most they would all come together and keep me together as my world was blown apart. But since that day, I had also begun picking up the pieces of myself and trying to constantly do right with them as to not make any mistakes that could bring me back down, bring anyone back down. I went directly to my default of trying to be righteous on my own.

"Read Romans," he said, "and we'll talk about what you see."

B efore college and marriage and motherhood, when we were all much younger and living together in the same home, my mother, sister, and I were frequent puzzle-putter-togetherers. Spread out on a table would be a large pile of pieces, and slowly, over a few days or hours if we were on a roll, as we gathered at the table on and off to relax in the art of puzzle piece placing, the picture would become clearer and the pieces would be easier to place as the pile grew smaller.

Recently I found out a sweet friend is, in fact, a puzzle aficionado. She shared with us through social media the way she solves a puzzle—the way she organizes, divides, and brings back together the thousands of pieces it takes to create the image appearing on the cover of the box. It was quite ingenious and made even the most intricate of pictures seem like a task that could very easily be conquered.

Somewhere between childhood and becoming an adult I began to think of the *big picture* God knew about me as one of those intricately huge puzzles with pieces spread all over, and like a scavenger hunt of experiences, I would have to keep an eye out for them, grab the ones I found, and then spread them on a table to try and piece them together and figure out what step was next in order to make that big picture a little bit clearer.

While learning from experiences and being open to God speaking through them is a wonderful way to learn valuable wisdom and insight, it's leaving out, as the *Jesus Storybook Bible* says, "the piece that makes all the other pieces fit together."[21]

Even with a heart very much in love with Jesus, I had put together, in my pre-bomb years, a worldview based on my own thoughts about what I had read, what I had been taught, what I had noticed others do or not do, what I deemed good or bad based on the effects it brought, all the while not understanding that I was making things much more difficult than they needed to be by blocking myself from the true meaning of the word that is now my greatest companion. In an effort to put together the puzzle, to see the next part of the picture, there was a lack of *abiding* in the work of Jesus alone. Honestly, saying there was a lack is much too tame a term. There was, in fact, an overwhelming desire to find righteousness on my own, to prove myself, to prove my worth.

Did I know I loved Jesus? Yes. Did I believe He was with me? Yes. Did I understand truly what it meant to put all of my faith in Him alone? No. Well, at least not permanently. I needed to comprehend the whole truth. I needed to find my faith. Actually, I needed faith to find me. And there it was, in the aftermath of the explosion, in the midst of facing hopelessness, understanding hope and learning to abide, that faith found me, again. It was there that it floated up and made itself visible. There it was, patiently waiting until I saw and realized that though it had never left, I had never let it come first.

> *"Therefore, since we have been justified by faith, we have peace with God through our Lord Jesus Christ. Through Him we have also obtained access by faith into this grace in which we stand, and we rejoice in hope of the glory of God. Not only that, but we rejoice in our sufferings, knowing that suffering produces endurance and endurance produces character and character produces hope and hope does not put us to shame because God's love has been poured into our hearts through the Holy Spirit who has been given to us."—Romans 5:1–5 (ESV)*

Our eternal lives in Christ, our lives in communion with the Father, start with faith. We were justified by faith, legally declared right before God and His law, not because of anything we did, not because we were able to pick up all of our pieces and arrange them into the picture that matched the puzzle box, but because of faith in Jesus produced in us by the Holy Spirit.

It all has to start somewhere. There is a beginning to reaching hope and it's not just recognizing hopelessness; something in us has to point us even to that. That "something" is the Spirit within us. That Spirit comes and works in our hearts, softens our hearts, and produces, slowly for some and in a flash for others, faith in the work of Jesus. Faith, this gift of God given by His great grace, is where each of our journeys as His children start, but it is also something our human hearts and minds forget, something our flesh tries really hard to rid us of. Faith is the beginning, and faith starts the chain reaction to hope.

Each of our three boys learned to ride their bikes in very different fashions, ones that match their overall personalities to a T. Our oldest learned gradually, methodically moving from one step to the other until he finally stopped freaking out long enough to realize he was really riding on his own. The video of his first ride is priceless, as he simultaneously screams at his dad to not let go of the bike and laughs out loud because he realizes he's riding on his own after his dad let go anyway.

Our middle decided one day that *that* was the day he was going for it and then pretty much jumped on the bike with minimal help and took off as if he had practiced the event so often in his head that he did not need actual practice in the physical world. Oh, to have his confidence and determination! They are the traits I admire in him the most.

Our youngest —oh, that baby—rocked his first time on two wheels. I was inside cleaning the kitchen when he came and told me he wanted to try his two-wheeler. Not even bothering to put on shoes, because this boy had cried wolf before, I very shortly found myself running barefoot down the street with our oldest videoing his first epic ride. However, the day after that first ride, and for many more, he claimed he did not know how to do it and refused to even try. It was not until his neighbor friend came over on two wheels and upon seeing the competition yelled, "Daddy, get my bike!" After that it was still an up-and-down experience because, bless his diva heart, if the conditions are not PERFECT, buckle up for a patience-draining trip around the block. Fast forward to now and he zooms down the street with ease and little regard to the safety of himself or anyone else.

I see myself so much in each of their scenarios, especially with regard to my faith. Whether it's methodically doing the right steps the right way so that the end result is practically perfect or jumping in with the confidence that I can get it done on my own or going down the trail trying, succeeding, fearing failure, quitting, and trying again, I am constantly being given ways to "work out my salvation with fear and trembling," as Paul writes in Philippians 2:12–13. (ESV) And yet, self-righteousness often rears its ugly head.

You see, if given my wish, my bike metaphor for faith would be *God, give me a push so that I can ride on my own from here.*

When thinking of the verse from Philippians, it was never the fear and trembling part I had a problem with, which is odd since that word *fear* usually is in my top five of describing myself. (Thankfully, somewhere in my teenage days it was explained to me that *fear* is really just a deep respect and *trembling* is understanding your weaknesses, which comes from humility. There's a little nugget of wisdom for you.) No, the problem I have always had is the *working* part, because what God always calls *working* I translate as *earning* instead.

Faith is a walk toward God with God. It is a working out, a struggle between flesh and Spirit as we initially believe and then begin the fight against our unbelief. It is not perfect, but within it we are being perfected. This is what sanctification is all about: a life-long process that continually shapes us to be more like Jesus; those ups and downs, bombs and recoveries that form us into whom we are meant to be, all the while needing to remember that none can truly shake us, none can bring us down, because through it all there is always hope.

Looking back over the years, three distinct stages of growing in faith have emerged. As you read through these, I pray

116

that my story disappears in your thoughts and your story comes alive within you so that you can either see yourself in one of these stages or be led to discern the ones that have marked your own life. In reading these examples, my prayer is that you won't be discouraged at any of your lacks, but instead be led to feel power in your weaknesses, leading you to hope in the growth that is promised. The hope that comes by faith coming first.

STAGE 1- PASSIVE FAITH

To be passive is basically to sit back and just let things happen to you. For reasons that would require an extensive explanation of my background that will not be shared here but will delightedly be shared with you personally over a cup of tea should you ever ask, there was a very long period of time where a passive view of faith led my life. While there have always been hints of self-righteous earning and the desire to be good and do good in hopes that that would up my status, so to speak, the majority of my life was spent thinking that faith was just something that happened to you; as in, "God gave us each a measure of faith"[22] and we were kind of stuck with how much we got and how much we could grow spiritually because of it.

That thought and a wrong interpretation of Romans 12:3 led me to sit motionless and uncaring at times, and at other times, caring too much and desperately seeking how to be okay with where I was. In neither occasion was I truly understanding that growth WAS possible and I am NEVER just stuck. The thing about trying to prove your righteousness on your own is that you seldom ask others for help. The thing about being an introverted person who is trying to prove their personal righteousness on their own means that not only do you seldom ask others for help, but you are so afraid of bothering another person that you don't just fight against asking because of pride, but now you have the added guilt brought on by personality. Stinking doubled-edged sword.

Thinking that no matter what I did either way would make any difference, I became equally content and discontent with my spiritual life in the midst of this passive faith.

STAGE 2: AGGRESSIVE FAITH

Next, as I entered my late twenties, I heard a sermon series on a spiritual disciplines that changed my spiritual life dramatically. I wish I could say it was a poignant moment, something like Paul when his blinded eyes began to see again in Acts 9, but it was really more like the ditzy blonde in a movie who finally gets the joke and begins to laugh after everyone else has already moved on. Regardless, my eyes were opened to truths and promises that I had never before understood, and there before me, in lists and notes, were ways and things I could do to grow. As a Type A, it was a dream come true. Read, meditate, pray, watch, fast, worship, memorize—all actions. YES! All tangibles that sent me from being a spectator of my faith to jumping in and doing something about it.

It was a time of amazing growth and learning, and it pre-pared my heart for the trials that would come just a few short years later. However, while this remains one of the most mem-orable times of being drawn close and being enlightened about what God has enabled us to do, in the background, it just fed that self-righteousness within. Creeping ever so consistently in was the thought that now that I have started, now that I have learned the ways of growing in God, I have to keep going. I have to work hard to make sure it continues. The gift of a new-found and growing faith was taken over as I mistook growing WITH God and all that He left for us in His Word and Spirit, to growing IN God of my own power. Those first moments of thankfulness began shifting instead into a personal triumph.

STAGE 3: ACTIVE PARTICIPATION

God does not need us to fulfill His plans. Honestly, they would probably work out much quicker if He did not let us be a part of them. As hard as that may be to hear, it is true.

Think of the times when you are trying to accomplish ANYTHING at your house, be it cleaning, cooking, laundry, car-washing, gardening, building, painting, or lawn-mowing, and your sweet little toddler comes up and asks if they can help. The job that would have taken you ten minutes has now taken you two hours, but in the process there was knowledge passed down, there was a connection made, and there was love poured out.

We are not powerful enough to destroy God's plans—and all the people said *Amen*—but we are also not holy enough to fulfill them. However, we are loved enough to be asked to participate in His kingdom for our own benefit, for the encouragement of others, and for His ultimate glory.

God invites us to participate with Him through the spiritual disciplines, through acting out and using our spiritual gifts, and through practicing the fruit of the Spirit. We are asked to participate so that we get a front-row seat to seeing Him work and love and grow and build and disciple and rescue. We get a front-row seat to the fulfilling of His promises so that we will learn to see His hand in every minute detail of life so that, instead of trying to go it alone, we burrow deeper into the shadow of His wing, abiding, knowing that is the only place to be.

The lesson in this stage is one I was missing in the first, the one that knows our faith can grow, just not of our own might. "Lord, thank you for our faith," John Piper prays. "Sustain it. Strengthen it. Deepen it. Don't let it fail. Make it the power of our lives, so that in everything we do you get the glory as the Great Giver."[23] He has the pieces to the puzzle, He knows by heart the picture on the box, and we get to crawl into His lap, take the piece He is holding, and place it where He leads so that the picture is revealed to us as well.

"However," Madeleine L'Engle said in *Circle of Quiet*, the first of her *Crosswicks Journals*, "even in the midst of pure thankfulness for an all-knowing and loving Father there is a human desire to know what's next, the direction of the next step, the ability 'to have a road map of exactly where we are going.'"[24]

Likewise, I wish I could say that I am currently entrenched in this Active Participation Stage, that I rejoice in the gift of faith given and the way in which it increases only through Christ. But, the world being broken as it is, I crawl away at times and just wait for things to happen or try again to ride on my own with nothing but a push. If you are actively participating in your faith, then lessons must be repeated. And I'm not a big fan of repetition.

During spring break of my junior year of college I took a road trip to New York with my now husband and two other guy friends. On the most budget-friendly (read *desperately frugal* because we were poor college students) NYC trip imaginable, we did anything and everything that was free and cheap. Therefore, we had to walk A LOT!

One day, as we were navigating the city, we realized the course we needed to take was exactly the same path as the day before. These three males I was with found it hilarious to also repeat every conversation and comment that was made the day before as well. Apparently, repetition is the key to comedy. I don't know about that. Repetition tends to be the key to unlocking all kinds of anger within my soul.

Efficiency is my favorite. My days revolve around what needs to get done, who needs to go where, and how it can be completed in the most efficient way possible. Days when I drive into the driveway after dropping the boys off at school only to discover a forgotten lunch box on the floor of the car make me seethe just a bit. Not because a child made a mistake, but because now instead of going straight into the house to begin the next thing, I have to turn around and go back and repeat the act I just completed.

I want to walk up a mountain and reach its peak. I want to start each day with everything just as I left it. I want to remember each lesson taught so the next day only holds new ones. I want God to just finish His work in me already so I can move on with my life. Yeah, that one stopped me in my tracks too.

The truth that the more we grow in faith the more we realize how much we need to grow in faith can be rough at times. He created us not only to constantly need Him but to desire to reach for Him as well, over and over, looking for His ways, not our own, seeing our weaknesses so that we ask for His strength. He created us for repetition, the repetition of dying to ourselves and relying on the faith we have been given in Christ, the righteousness that comes through Him and only Him.

Author and blogger Lara Williams wrote, "We cannot coast today on yesterday's faith."[25] Yes, yesterday's faith taught us lessons. Yes, yesterday's faith drew us closer; but our human hearts, chock full of the *black stuff*, as my youngest calls it, are always trying to take over. Paul Tripp reminds us that, "Sin renders us unable."[26] We need help, and on the daily, in every aspect of our lives. Faith bears repeating.

It is this knowledge of faith coming first, being entrenched in the understanding of trusting God with each step and circumstance, and needing repeated lessons of that faith that eventually leads to hope. As the verse in Romans says, in between those two elements of faith and hope are suffering, endurance, and character. Those three things are otherwise known as your individual life story.

The *sufferings* you have known, the *endurance* you have developed, and the *character* that has been built within makes you who you are. Faith will guide you to embrace all facets of your own story, because you will see how each thing produces another, and then another, that leads you to the hope that does not put you to shame because love has been poured out all along the way.

My story is important. Your story is important. Our stories are important. All of our stories. Every single story and every single detail of them. Why? Because God is the author of them all and nothing He does is wasted. He is a part of all the little things and all the big things and all the seemingly insignificant things in between.

Have faith that your life was created with meaning and purpose, each little part, and do not be afraid to tell it in big places and in small. He placed you in His story because He created your story to matter. "Beautiful are the ways of God if we allow

Him to use us as he wants."[27] This quote from Mother Teresa
has a life of hard and beauty behind it. A woman, known and
loved by the masses with a story.

It's easy to look back and see all that is lacking, to doubt
that anything done could have made an impression on others,
or to look forward and continue to doubt that there is something great and special on the horizon. You and I are not the
only ones to see the faults glaring brighter than the gifts, but
you and I both hold the promise that gifts are exactly what we
have been given (Ephesians 1:3), and a hope and a future are
there for us as well. (Jeremiah 29:11)

We often assume good things only come from big important places or big important people. When there are 7 billion
people available, some are going to be well-known, famously
or infamously so. Most of us, however, will not reach that level
of recognition by the masses, but that doesn't mean we don't
each have an important story to tell. We each have the ability to
impact another with what we have been through, what we have
been brought through, and where we are going.

There is a verse in John that portrays a similar precon-
ceived opinion that one of the disciples had before following
along when called. Philip tells his friend Nathanael that they
have found the Messiah and are going to follow him. His friend
replies in John 1:46, "Can anything good come out of Nazareth?" (ESV)

Oh, Nazareth, you precious little blip on the map, can good
from you? Yes, and it was the ultimate good.

Just as Sally Lloyd Jones tells us in her *Jesus Storybook Bible*
that "every story of the Bible whispers His name,"[28] our lives
do the same. But sometimes, as Brennan Manning wrote, "in
a futile attempt to erase our past, we deprive the community

of our healing gift. If we conceal our wounds out of fear and shame, our inner darkness can neither be illuminated nor become a light for others."[29]

There is such beauty in sharing your life to benefit the life of another. And there is beauty in letting faith in your Creator, Savior, and His Spirit envelop your life so that same faith can enable you to shine in the darkness.

But you cannot tell a story that you don't remember and you can't see God's hand in a story that you don't acknowledge. So, a word of advice, write it down, and then read it over and over. Let it show you where you have been and where you are now, and believe that you are not yet where you will be.

During our first post-bomb counseling session, our pastor encouraged us to each get a notebook and write down everything. Everything we were thinking, feeling, learning, saying, wanting to say. EVERYTHING. No, journaling is not a command from God, but where would we be now without the words others had journaled throughout history? The law, the letters, the gospels, the Bible as a whole were words written down for one person's remembrance or for sharing with a group, and those now provide us with the ability to know our Creator and see His hand throughout eternity.

That journal that still sits on my nightstand doesn't just contain my ramblings and feelings. It contains those Scriptures that leapt off the pages as I poured through His Word. It contains prayers written through tears as I was mining my heart. It contains the idols I could see in my own life and needed to destroy. It contains the joys of getting over the next hurdle. It contains the story of the first year of healing and it shows the road I was taken on and, most importantly, it glows with the faithfulness of my Father.

As you look back at your life, as you write down your story, every piece you can remember from the beginning to present day, you have also written down the faithfulness of God in your life—the sufferings that came, the endurance those experiences built, the character they produced, and the hope that vibrantly shone at the end of each.

This part is where the *working out* comes into play. It's the one-on-one wrestling with God through your story, through your own walk in faith, through your initial belief and your fight against unbelief. Hope is produced through exercising faith by reading His Word, through exercising faith in conversation with Him in prayer, and by exercising faith by writing down your story and seeing Him throughout it. Hope rises to visible heights and is no longer hidden behind the fence or blocked by fear and distractions and idols. Hope reveals itself to have been with us all along, because Christ has been with us all along.

When you tell those stories out loud for the benefit of another and when you live those stories in public and let them speak for themselves, lives are changed. But the most important person your story is for is you, because one of those days will come that will drive you into forgetting it all and wanting to throw it all away. That is where the hope gained through it all does its work, as we see not just hopelessness, but the hope that came after.

In the midst of one of *those days*, my husband texted me the very verse we began this chapter with and have been repeating throughout, along with the rhetorical question, *Why can we not just get hope first, why the process?* As I took that trail to the end in my mind, I settled on one word: *Because.*

Because is a word that can be both explanatory and exasperating, full of peace and resolve or full of questions and frustration.

Because, sometimes things happen. Because, even if we do not understand it, there is no answer other than God is the creator and author of the universe. Because, His ways are not our ways and His thoughts not our thoughts. (Isaiah 55:8–9) Because, He can work all things together for good. (Romans 8:28) Because, He knows the whole story and we are only privy to one small part at a time. Because, He gets to say.

The good news is, faith came first, and our faith in Him lets us live in those times of *because*, because through that faith we have obtained access to grace and can rejoice in the HOPE of His glory.

In his book *Jayber Crow*, Wendell Berry wrote this:

> "'You have been given questions to which you cannot be given answers. You will have to live them out, perhaps a little at a time.'
> 'And how long is that going to take?'
> 'I don't know. As long as you live, perhaps.'
> 'That could be a long time.'
> 'I will tell you a further mystery.' he said. 'It may take longer.'"[30]

That will not always be the case; answers at times are quite clear. But even when they are not, our eternal lives in Christ, our communion with the Father, still starts with faith. Faith started it all, and led to rejoicing in all things, including sufferings which lead to perseverance, which leads to character, which leads to hope.

In hope is where we stay, in hope is where we cling, and as we rest there, this hope has so much to bring.

7

Hope Brings

Trapped on a merry-go-round. That is precisely how I felt pre-bomb. Friendships were feeling off, marriage was feeling off, communication, parenting, church, myself, you name it. This festering secret being held by two others had weaseled its way through my entire life without my really knowing, except for the side effect of the emotional spinning I felt because of it all. I could never really pinpoint the one thing or maybe didn't want to admit that I had pinpointed the one thing, so instead I just felt a sense of whirling around my life with everything blurred before me. I couldn't focus on any one part, but I was afraid of jumping off, so there I was, hanging on to the bars for dear life while it all just went faster and faster and faster.

Then, in one swift move, God reached down through time and space and with His violent love stopped the spinning in its tracks and sent every part of life flinging out in different directions. Slowing it down seems like it would have been easier. Slowing it down would have enabled my heart rate to lower peacefully, would have given me an opportunity to gather my bearings before getting off; but, inevitably, slowing it down would have also given me the chance to pack up all the baggage of uncertainty and take it with me again.

There Is Always Hope

I needed to see Him destroy it all in an instant so that I could also see Him piece it all back together. One sentence of an admission of guilt brought everything crumbling down, but one word, HOPE, began to put everything He wanted back together again. Like a run of dominoes, one small block starts a chain reaction. I have started many with my own sinful flesh, and I have been knocked over in the middle by others' actions, but I have learned to see the best ones are brought on by hope. That one word brings so much.

Someone once asked me, if I could pick any three fictional characters to put together to make a new me, who would I want them to be? Mary Poppins was on my list because of her no-nonsense, cheery disposition, but also because of her ability to carry so much around with her in one bag and her talent for cleaning an entire room with the snap of her fingers. Marvel Comics' Thanos could have used a lesson from her about how to make good use of a finger snap.

Next was Beatrice Prior from the book (and now movie) *Divergent* and its subsequent sequels. Not only would I love to carry the characteristics of a well-rounded person instead of being trapped in the box of one character quality, but having the ability to kick a little tail when needed wouldn't break my heart.

First place, however, goes to Kathleen Kelly, a.k.a. Meg Ryan's character in the movie *You've Got Mail*. I wanted to be her. I wanted her job, her apartment, her haircut, the ability to wear a trench coat and look adorable even when I'm sick. I'll confess, I definitely didn't want her mom jeans, but no one's perfect.

I've seen the movie too many times to count and while the

technology in it is most definitely antiquated, my *old millennial* labeling, or *Xennials* as they now call our small random group in between Gen Xers and millennials, means I will always carry a fondness in my heart for AOL instant messenger, its beautiful start-up sound, and the feeling of butterflies that dial-up internet brought to my teenage heart.

My favorite thing about Kathleen, hands-down, is the way she not only feels emotions, but expresses them. She is able to articulate feelings into words with such perception. One such example describes the feeling of change and how it disrupts our incredible love of comfort.

"People," she says as she mourns the loss of the work she has always known, "are always telling you that change is a good thing. But all they are really saying is that something you didn't want to happen at all, has happened."[31]

My heart hurts as I dwell on those words, because I know the feelings change can bring. The confused, hopeless feelings we're trying to pinpoint, call out, and bring hope straight into. There, are, right now, countless people sitting at the bottom of hopelessness due to changes they did not foresee—changes that are direct reflections of their negative choices, changes that are direct reflections of other people's negative choices, changes they do not know what to do with, or changes that seem incapable of bringing anything better into their lives or hearts. But change, as the "people" say, IS a good thing, or should I say, CAN be a good thing, if you see the ways that change is ushered in, wrapped up in the hope of what will be. Hope brings so many *wonderfuls* into our lives and hearts, and change is one of them.

HOPE BRINGS LIFE CHANGES

For reasons undoubtedly learned in college child-development classes but forgotten along the way, we've found in our parenting experience that age four is when imaginations begin to soar. Anything and everything can happen simply by pretending it to be so. When our oldest was four, he was thoroughly enthralled with a Flash costume. This thrift-store find was far from mint condition, but despite its loosening seams, hanging threads, and lack of ability to close in the back, to him it held the power to transport him, quite literally, in a *flash* anywhere his super powers were needed. Over and over I would watch as he zoomed past me from the hallway, constantly telling me I couldn't see him because he was going too fast.

One day, his daddy took a picture using an open shutter and created a blur of color where our little superhero zoomed by so that he could see that he really was just a flash.

I wish all flashes produced the smiles that boy had when he looked at that picture.

If you asked people around you, whether strangers on the street or your closest friends, what they fear, you will get a variety of answers. If you take out that list of fears you wrote down for yourself way back in chapter four and compared them, a common theme will arise: *fear of change.* We don't like change. We like same, predictable, normal. We like to feel cozy and comfortable, remember?

Even the unpleasant known is much more comforting than the potentially pleasant unknown. This mindset we've all surrendered to at times means we will sit in situations we don't want to be in and we will hold on to situations we don't like to be a part of, because at least we know what to expect, at least we can't get lost if we stay where we are. How confusing our human minds can be. What we need is the boldness to break out, the assurance that comes through faith and brings about the hope that 2 Corinthians 3:12 says makes us bold! But instead we're tempted to stay, staring down changes as they come and fearing what they will bring.

As I sat on that figurative merry-go-round, jumping off—which would have meant having the courage to speak up about the many parts of life that weren't working the way they should have and confronting my husband about the suspicions I had—never really crossed my mind. I preferred dealing with the pleasant known rather than the unknown that would have come. Hanging on for dear life and making the best of the constant whirling was the only answer that made sense to me. But God had a different opinion.

One of my favorite quotes is from *Flabbergasted*, written by Ray Blackston. "We spend vast amounts of time and energy crafting a thesis in our heads of how life should play out and then Almighty God spends an incredibly brief amount of time blowing our thesis to bits."[32] My thesis was definitely blown to bits.

For all of us, life is lived so often in flashes, small changes that appear and disappear in random order as we seek to find our way. Like a squirrel finding its way across a raging river by stepping on and leaping to whatever rock or tree trunk happens to be peeking above the surface until they have reached the other side, the bits and pieces of our days can also feel separate from each other, just bits of stone and wood that we leap to so we don't fall into the water below. The beauty comes in looking back and seeing that those bits and pieces were actually a jagged path leading you safely to the other shore.

At other times, though, the small flashes are not what we need. Instead, what we need is the violent love of an earth-shattering life explosion that separates your plan from God's, your human desires from His perfect ones, until the wake of that produces a greater beauty in the end, and you see what was once destroyed get built back up with the beauty of hope.

Looking back, it's crystal clear that the journey to make-believe was a needed experience in my boys' lives, as it is for the life of any child. Not only does it create grand memories for child and parent alike, but it opens minds and hearts to ideas outside of their tangible environment, ideas that would prepare them to be able to trust and have faith in something bigger than themselves, bigger than their understanding, bigger than their realm of possibility. Changes in our adult lives produce the same results.

Change is scary, but unless change happens, there can be nothing new, nothing exciting, and certainly no growth. Our bomb sparked big changes. All isn't roses and rainbows, many scars still remain and many idols are still being unearthed, because while I believe when Paul says that He who began a good work in me is faithful to complete it, I know that the completion phase can be a lifelong project. Regardless of what still needs to come, my heart has been changed from the inside out. While it's still being renewed daily, this heart has a new trajectory and a clearer purpose that would not have been possible without the initial change, without the thing I did not want to happen happening.

In flashes of His goodness, reminders of His faithfulness, and visible snapshots of grace and mercy, hope brings a variety of change and with it the exciting newness of a relationship found in Christ. "Therefore," it says in 2 Corinthians 5:17, "if anyone is in Christ, the new creation has come: The old has gone, the new is here." (NIV)

Yes, there were changes in life, but the hope that came brought LIFE CHANGE!

Any good that is here for me and for you doesn't come on our own terms or by our own hands. It's something we aren't able to create but is instead masterfully created. Therefore, we need not fear it. Corrie Ten Boom speaks directly to this when she challenges us to "never be afraid to trust an unknown future to a known God."

The changes that bombs bring into our lives are significant, but hope makes its way in and covers those difficult changes with goodness and doesn't just bring a needed change in our lives, but a life change through our hearts. Hope changes our hearts on the inside, and our hearts are then able to change the way we view the outside.

HOPE BRINGS A CHANGE OF VIEW

It's tempting to take newness and change in two different, yet harmful, ways. Depending on personality or prior knowledge of the change that is to come, one way is to attempt it all at once. The other is to attempt to hide from it completely. There is the typical battle within of getting it all over with, getting it all checked off, versus avoiding the need to begin with and doubting that any change is coming or even necessary. How often do we drift to one extreme or the other when there is a middle ground of patient faithfulness where we should usually be treading? For me, this drifting to extremes can happen daily.

Living in my home, and in yours as well, are minds that, as Paul Tripp puts it, "want to make life all about us, to want little more than our own way, and to live like little self-sovereigns."[33] Try as I might to just assume this is a trait my children have, I must stop trying to convince myself that there are just three young monarch wannabes walking the floors of our home. If I'm honest, there's a tendency to be queen in me as well. My heart desires my own way more often than it desires anyone else's. Sin clouds my vision. My eyes are always looking at something, but where are they actually focusing? What is my view?

Mr. Tushman, principal in the book *Wonder*, said, "Auggie can't change the way he looks, so maybe we can change the way we see."[34] Like Auggie, there is much about our lives we cannot change. As much as we are able to choose on our own through careful thought or wild abandon, control is something we have never been given, no matter how strongly we fight to take it anyway. The reason for this is the most loving thing I can think of: if we have the ability to control, our view will remain focused on ourselves, on what we want, and what we have to do to get it. Eyes lost in themselves will always be lost.

Truth and beauty lie beyond our limited vision. It is with the eyes of Christ that light can flood in and enable us to truly see. "The eye is the lamp of the body; so then if your eye is clear, your whole body will be full of light," says Matthew 6:22. (ESV) Our humanity isn't able to comprehend our view of this world that has been perfectly and divinely created; it is only with the newness of life through Christ, our gift of hope, that the fuzzy begins to turn clear.

Year ago, in my days of teaching, the principal frequently talked about paradigm shifts, a change in how you view a person or a situation that results in a change of approach. Within each believer, led by the Spirit within, is the ability to shift. Like an artist in the midst of capturing their imagination on canvas, we sometimes need just a slightly different angle, a bit of a head tilt to see what is truly there and what is the core essential for life. You don't always have to walk a mile down the road. It can just take a step or two to get a different view, but hope must be at the center as we take those steps.

It is this revived notion of hope, this understanding of our capability to live in the present, knowing that the promises of the future were earned by Christ in the past, that make the steps possible. And those steps guide our eyes to the light found within every situation. That light is our goal; actually, it's God's goal. He gave His Son as a sacrifice, and that Son gave us His Spirit as a guide, so that in every single situation in life, from the smallest bumps to the biggest bombs, our view would stay put, would be strictly focused on Christ and the hope He brings, regardless of what is falling down around us.

There are times when this is a little more daunting, and it's not just our flesh we're fighting against, but the physical effects change itself has made in our minds.

Change is inevitable and whether welcomed with open arms or fought against tooth and nail, it happens constantly. But it's not really the change itself that is the problem. Change is getting a bad rap. What we are uncomfortable with is things happening that we don't like, that we did not plan for ourselves, and the unknowns they bring. What we hate is when those things happen with no warning, because one of the hardest times you will ever face is when change sneaks up on you, unexpected, and then in a flash your normal is not only different, but you know it will never be the same again.

When someone, either just once or over and over,

experiences a figurative bomb going off in their lives, it may not bring the physical destruction a wire and metal bomb can, but it can definitely leave an emotional and spiritual aftermath of distress, confusion, and upheaval that can take just as long or even longer to recover from.

Inside your brain new pathways are created that now lead to distress, fear, anger, and a whole other host of negative emotions, which can then lead to the ending feeling of hopelessness. Because of these new pathways, any moment in the future that even hints at a past difficulty causes the sequence to trigger, and in less time than it takes to blink, your heart and mind are overcome with these new emotions that the past has created.

If, by chance, the trigger itself takes you by complete surprise in the midst of a happy moment, the journey to distress feels even more immediate, hitting you deeper, and the aftermath lasts longer, because the sense of normalcy you thought you had found again ended up being a farce. That doubt has the ability to grow like a weed until your confidence is so shaken that any happy moment is tread upon with rejection at worst and reluctance at best.

During a sermon, my father-in-law asked if any of us felt like we were experts in any given skill, and then he shared that in Malcolm Gladwell's book *Outliers*, Gladwell suggests that it takes 10,000 hours of deliberate practice to become an expert at something.[35] Often feeling like a jack-of-all trades, master-of-none, the pitiful list in my head was nothing to be impressed with.

However, in the years following the most significant bomb in my life so far, I feel as if I am coming up on pro status of understanding triggers and the difficulties they can cause in someone's day, and while that seems like a not-so-fun expertise, it is truly a gift that only hope can bring.

As you identify hopelessness in your life and what is blocking your way of finding hope, as you understand what hope truly is and how it comes through abiding in Christ, and as you let your faith start your journey instead of relying on yourself to power through, hope begins to place those experiences of change into the middle parts between suffering and hope.

PTSD is not reserved for one group of people; life can be a war zone as your flesh and spirit consistently battle and as the traumas you face affect you in deep ways. As you grow and are able to remember your experience without reliving it, the pathways these life bombs built to cause distress become the pathways straight to hope instead. Hope, as it reminds you again and again of its ability to bring about a better future surrounded by the comfort of Christ, begins to calm the triggers until they either disappear or bring about a new emotional result at the end.

Whether the shift comes with a mere head tilt to achieve a slightly different perspective or a long road through trauma, hope centers our view, like a laser focused on the peace that comes from a stayed mind in Christ. It is a pinhole in the middle of the paper that we can peek through and see, truly see, what is real. It's there. I promise with every ounce of my being that hope resides within the darkest places. But when my promises mean nothing, focus on the One who does mean something, the One who has told us to hold on to the hope set before us, because that's our anchor, and it will keep us steady and unshaken as the seas calmly roll beneath us or try to shatter us upon the rocks. (Hebrews 6:19) Abiding there and clinging to hope helps us see, lifts us past the fence, sets our minds and eyes above, no matter what is going on around or below.

"The eyes of my heart have been enlightened," Ephesians 1:18 says, "and I know the Hope he has called me to." (NIV) Hope changes both our view and the ability to see our view differently. We look now from His eyes, the eyes that see it all, and as we look with His eyes and not our own, we begin to see the people all around that He has given as gifts in our times of need, because hope brings community.

Hope Brings Community

"Two are better than one, because they have a good return for their labor: If either of them falls down, one can help the other up. But pity anyone who falls and has no one to help them up. Also, if two lie down together, they will keep warm. But how can one keep warm alone? Though one may be overpowered, two can defend themselves. A cord of three strands is not quickly broken."—Ecclesiastes 4:9–12 (NIV)

We were created to long for something other than ourselves. We were created to share our thoughts and our hearts, our time and space, our burdens and our joys with others, because two are better than one. If you fall, one will lift up their fellow. Forrest and Bubba knew this as they leaned against each other so they wouldn't have to sleep with their faces in the mud. Woody knew this as he told all the toys to make sure to get their moving buddies ready at the beginning of *Toy Story*. Your elementary teacher knew this as he or she partnered you off before a field trip to make sure someone was looking out for you as you looked out for them. Jesus knew this as He sent the seventy-two disciples out in pairs to do their work. Though they could take nothing else with them, they still had each other, because He knew that besides His Gospel message, community was what they needed most.

Unfortunately, Satan also knows how much we need each other, which is why he does his best to convince us that we are all alone. In our struggles, in our sins, in our everyday lives, he plants in us lies and triggers our insecurities to keep us from doing what is best for us: leaning on others. Apart from convincing us that we do not need God, he also attempts to convince us that we do not need anyone but ourselves. And even beyond that, he attempts to convince us that others are so much the same way that even if we did reach out, they wouldn't reach back.

How do I know this? Because it has been a common storyline in my life since I can remember. My own fears and doubts have affected my relationships for the majority of my life. Even when it seemed obvious to others that there were people placed right by my side, Satan would use those doubts, not that I was physically alone but that I was emotionally so, to make me feel unloved or unwanted. *They only need you because of your skill and productivity. They are using you for your gifts. They don't really want to be around you. They don't really want to be your friend.* He knew the doubts I held inside, he understood my self-righteousness tendencies and needing to get it right on my own, and he watered it all and watched it grow tall so that those evil weeds could try and block out the good, flowering fruit below.

Then the bomb came. The hand grabbed the bar of the merry-go-round. The violent love of my Creator forced those lies to be exposed and let me slide the whole way down to hopelessness so that when I looked up I didn't just see Him, I saw the people He had so lovingly given me and the ones He would begin to give me to take the burden, to walk alongside me, to be the body of Christ that functions as one, however big or small the part.

One of my favorite stories in the Bible is told in Mark 2:1–12 and in two other gospels—Matthew and Luke. Jesus was speaking at someone's home and a few men, knowing the power of this man everyone was talking about, brought their paralyzed friend to the house, confident that Jesus could heal him. When they got there the crowd was so big that they couldn't get anywhere close to the door. No worries. Instead of giving up, they crawled on top of the roof, cut a hole in the thatch, and lowered their friend inside, right to the feet of Jesus.

There are multiple lessons to be learned from this story, but the one I want you to focus on now is the man's relationship with his friends. It's not just that this man had awesome friends—because seriously, those were some dedicated bros—who wanted him to get better. This man had awesome friends because they took him straight to Jesus. They loved him so much that they risked a lot—embarrassment, injury, rejection, the repercussions of ruining someone's home—to take him to the only One that mattered. They pointed him, quite literally, straight to the Savior.

Christ is over all things. In Colossians 1:16 we read that, "For by Him all things were created, in heaven and on earth, visible and invisible, whether thrones or dominions or rulers or authorities. All things were created through Him and for Him and He is before all things and in Him all things hold together." (ESV) He was sent to dwell on this earth because He is over all things and because we are not and can't ever be.

We, as finite beings, were created for community, created to work together, to pick up where others leave off and to accomplish tasks another was not created to accomplish. Romans 12:4 states, "For just as each of us has one body with many members, these members do not all have the same function." (NIV) All of us collectively make up what our one individual Savior was able to do on His own.

When we seek out people to be in community with, we often try way too hard to find those who have similar interests, those who look *cool* and would be fun to go out with, or those who always tell us we're justified in whatever feelings we have and pat us on the back and say it will be okay no matter what the situation. While most of those qualities are fine and fun to have, they do not mean much with regards to real Gospel community. The most important question is *Will they point us to Jesus?* When we need it most, will they cut a hole in the roof and lower us down to the only One who can help?

Dietrich Bonhoeffer wrote an insightful book about Christian community called *Life Together.* In it, Bonhoeffer helps believers know and understand what it means to live in community and how to actively live in this way. It is one of the best books I have ever had the pleasure to read. Within the first page there is an astounding statement, "It is not simply to be taken for granted that the Christian has the privilege of living among other Christians."[36]

Not everyone has the opportunity to surround themselves with believers. Many don't even have the opportunity to freely express their belief so that they may find like-minded individuals to commune with. The early church, detailed in the book of Acts, is a beautiful picture of Christian community. They devoted themselves to one another, working together, eating together, praying together, selling their possessions if they had too much to help a brother who was falling on hard times.

It isn't easy to reach out past doubts and insecurities, past fears and assumptions, to become part of other people's lives. There are many of us who have to climb over many things, including personality differences, to seek out the community around us. Introverts tend to hold a small amount of people dear to them and occasionally miss deep relationship with another because of the exhaustion that comes with forming just one more relationship. Extroverts tend to talk to everyone and can occasionally miss deep relationships because they are trying to please all.

The good thing is, there is no minimum for community, and there is also no cap. As long as you are resting in Christ, believing confidently in hope, knowing that God has kept His promises of the future while living in the present because of what Jesus did for you in the past, you can be assured that through hope in Christ, He will provide the relationships meant specifically for you and for whom you were also meant specifically.

Remember that first text message I received—the one about rejoicing, hoping, resting, and being satisfied in the Lord alone? The more we are satisfied in the Lord alone, the more people will be drawn to us in community, because we aren't afraid to seek them out for fear they will not be able to fill in us our basic needs. When the Lord is supplying your basic needs, your community only needs to be there to walk with you, remind you where to look, and hold your arms up when you grow tired. Through the obedience of Moses holding up his arms in Exodus 17:12–14, God destroyed the enemy. Moses didn't need his friends to fight the war; he just needed them to help him obey the One who could.

As we grow closer to God through hope in His Son, we become better at being friends to others, at being their community. Bonhoeffer also says, "He who loves his dream of a community more than the Christian community itself becomes a destroyer of the latter."[37] When filling up your spiritual cup with Christ instead of using friendships to get what you need, you begin going into those relationships with a mindset of giving what others need. You are there to serve, not to be served. To be a light. When all those around you are doing this same thing, a beautiful representation of the Gospel takes place.

"The more genuine and the deeper our community becomes, the more will everything else between us recede, the more clearly and purely will Jesus Christ and his work become the one and only thing that is vital between us," Dietrich Bonhoeffer says.[38]

Hope brings community with people around you, pointing you to Jesus in the biggest and smallest of ways, allowing you to point others to Him as well. As that hope brings community to you, that community in turn brings your attention to hope, bringing more dependence on hope as you grow in Christ. This is a merry-go-round I don't mind spinning on.

Yes, change occurs. Yes, in the midst of change you may find yourself in a state of chaos, and while that chaos around you might never change, inside the bullseye, the ground zero of your specific circumstance, hope comes in and brings order. Hope makes sense of the nonsensical, because as changes in life happen, hope changes your view and brings people around you to lean against while they lean back. But hope does not stop there.

Through the character Jayber Crow, Wendell Berry says, "Telling a story is like reaching into a granary full of wheat and drawing out a handful. There is always more to tell than can be told."[39] That is what a life in hope is like. There is always more being added to the story, always more ways you are being made new through Him, always changes that are happening. But always, hope is in the middle to guide us through it all.

8
When You Want to Give Up

It was after a peaceful day together, children in bed, plans made to just sit and watch a movie that would relax us into sleep, when the offhand comment was made. We all do it, all the time. We say random things that to us mean very little but to others carry enough weight to knock them over. This comment was a weighty one, and I crumbled under it. After months of healing souls and growing relationships, after months of learning to be vulnerable and having us both blossom under that, was one comment really going to derail it all? In my mind, in that instant, those few words changed so much and with that change came flooding back the exhaustive feelings of the very beginning. I cannot do this again. I cannot walk through all of this again. Square one is too far to fall.

In a huddled heap I sobbed, seriously ready to throw in the towel, wrapped in the arms of a man who was desperately trying to understand what on earth he had said that garnered the reaction that was manifesting before him. Me trying to formulate words within the emotion to explain why it was so upsetting wasn't working this time. I didn't want to have to explain; I was tired of explaining.

Glancing up to see an innocent conversation happening nearby at church, being tagged in a Facebook post, making a quick trip to Target all posed unexpected danger zones; there were many times this feeling of exhaustion came up. Many days that felt like a reboot, like life had suddenly frozen and needed to be turned off and then back on again. Many days that fright and flight overpowered the desire to stand up and fight. The majority of post-bomb days moved me forward, either leaping, running, or trudging through the mud, but still with forward progress. But alongside those were others that sent me reeling. Yes, they thankfully were few and far between; yes, they only lasted a small amount of time in comparison. But they were still there, pulling me down, making me rethink or making me not want to think at all. These were the days when I just wanted to give up.

"How is faith to endure, O God, when you allow all this scraping and tearing on us? You have allowed rivers of blood to flow, mountains of suffering to pile up, sobs to become humanity's song—all without lifting a finger that we could see. You have allowed bonds of love beyond number to be painfully snapped. If you have not abandoned us explain Yourself. We strain to hear, but instead of hearing an answer we catch sight of God himself scraped and torn. Through our tears we see the tears of God."
—*Nicholas Wolterstorff,* Lament for a Son[40]

The days will come when all of it is just too much. When hopeless tries to fight its way back into your heart and convince you that all the gains you have made are nothing but a farce. When hopeless tries to convince you that the hope that was reigning in your life is worthless, that hope is a lie that came from ignorance, and that you are truly no better off than you were at the beginning.

It would be easy to write the words *don't give up, it will all be worth it*, but in those moments, words are not what you need. Patience is all that can be given. When you find yourself in that place, in the place of being done, of wanting it all to just be over and disappear, of thinking that the only way to fix anything is to give up and walk away, the first thing you need to be given is patience. And then, you just need to wait.

But just because your soul needs to wait does not mean your feet have to. Find your spot, your space that allows breathing to reconvene at its normal pace. Don't run away and hide; run to and sit. Let your thoughts flow out, write them down like we talked about earlier, or let them filter out on their own. Follow those thoughts to the end of your deepest fears and see the worst that can happen. Through that practice of sitting and waiting, let the lessons of hope you have fought hard to learn and the lessons of hope that have been graciously given to you wash over you and bring you peace.

Wait until your heart rate goes back down; wait until the anger subsides; wait until the grief that violently washed in slowly washes back out again. The truths you have learned will float up. They'll enter your mind and your heart. They did not run away, so you do not have to either. See hope remain; let hope remain.

This moment you are feeling right now, this one triggered by a comment, a scenario, a picture, social media, or an uninvited flashback in your mind, this moment is also held up with hope. This moment, as difficult as it is, is no different from the many others that line up in life between suffering and hope. This moment is an attempt by the evil one to break you, to turn you around, causing you to lose your way. This moment is his attempt to try to make you feel alone, lied to, or unprotected. It is meant to make you give up.

I know Someone whose desire is for you to know you can always keep going because there is always hope. I know Someone who creates beauty in the darkest places. I know Someone whose creation screams out loveliness no matter how much ugly tries to fight its way in. I know Someone who divinely places people and situations in our lives that have the gift of noticing and who help us learn to pay attention as well. One such gift this Someone gave me came in the form of a fictional redhead.

Anne Shirley from *Anne of Green Gables* occupies a very large and precious place in my heart. A love for this spunky character was born when I was young by the side of one of my best and oldest friends, and it has deepened my relationships with others because of our ability to find kindred spirits in one another through a mutual love of these tales. When re-reading the entire series recently, I was drawn even more to Anne's ability to see beauty wherever she went. "'What a splendid day!' said Anne. 'Isn't it good just to be alive on a day like this? I pity the people who aren't born yet for missing it.'"[41]

If I was to imagine a day like the one to which she was referring, it would be one with a bright blue sky, a smattering of white clouds with a hint of a breeze, and a fully shining sun. It would, of course, be void of the normal Georgia humidity and would, without a doubt, have a beach or mountain or garden or field or city skyline for a view, depending on preference at the time. It would also be one where everything seems to fall into place and where the only thing left to do is enjoy it.

Maybe these days happen, but then again there is a reason why *Alexander and the Terrible, Horrible, No Good, Very Bad Day* has been a significant part of children's literature for over forty years. Because as much as we may want to avoid crappy days, "some days are like that, even in Australia."[42]

There are days with unbearable heat that have you searching for cool air wherever you can find it, days with painful cold that send people huddling indoors or struck with fear about how to stay warm when there's no door to go *in*, days with rain and fog and gray-clouded dreariness that affects the mood without any effort. There are also days where the outside weather may be textbook perfect, but your heart is feeling something so different inside that your eyes have trouble seeing the beauty for what it is and, more importantly, from where and from Whom it comes.

One of my greatest skills is envisioning and creating tangible beauty, deciding what would look best in any given place or within any opportunity. Whether it's exterior home projects, landscaping, interior design, decorating projects for friends, refinishing furniture, or just ways to fill up free days with the family at home, there is always an ideal in my head of how life, both the living of it and the visual around it, would look best.

On the flip side, one of my greatest triggers of frustration is when these lovely, perfectly imagined ideals do not play out properly. Perfecting ideals has its place. Planning, organizing, and imagining how to create beauty and give beauty to others is a responsibility of ours as stewards of this world God created. "I have given you dominion over it," He said in Genesis. We must take care. When our perfect ideal that we conjure up inside, however, masks the reality that is playing out, we are not seeing or showing true beauty.

Through this season, this post-bomb-rebuilding-being-rebuilt time of life, beauty should have been so hard to find, should have felt like a desperate daily search just to dig up an ounce to cling to. And as those days came up, those days so filled with triggers that I would have gladly given up rather than walk through them again, I was met instead with arrows shooting straight through my cloudy vision to the small beautiful things forever in the midst. He pierced the darkness that I saw with pricks of light, one arrow at a time, one small thankfulness at a time, and pointed them out to me in ways only the Lord can do, until the things that once had been stared right through became beacons in the rubble.

The inability of projects and circumstances to reach my planned expectations might feel like a failure at the time, but truly they are gracious reminders that I do not need perfection around me, that I can find beauty anywhere and through anything. This understanding can only be an accomplishment of hope. However beautiful the schemes seemed in my head, the beauty revealed through everything covered in Christ is beauty unsurpassed.

Hope tells us that beauty exists because of what Christ has done for us. Our ability to live peacefully in the present, with a fulfilling future to come, because of His sacrifice in the past, does not disappear and then reappear when conditions are perfect. Beauty is not based on circumstances.

Beauty can be seen and found in any and all times, through each and every scenario the world brings, because it is wholly dependent upon the view through which you are looking. Hope picks us up over the fence, remember? Hope clears our vision. Hope gives us eyes to see life based on Christ's righteousness, not our own. There is no shortage of things we are promised when we cling to our God of Hope, and while those promises never include perfect lives, they always include life given from

One who did live perfectly. One such promise is found in Isaiah 61:3: "To all who mourn . . . He will give a crown of beauty for ashes, a joyous blessing instead of mourning, festive praise instead of despair." (NLT)

The juxtaposition of beauty and despair is a constant for us all. The scales dip from one side to another, staying down at times longer than anyone would wish, or staying up so long that the next dip down catches us by surprise more than it should.

Growing up you learn in school about how America came to be and its beautiful melting pot of colors, faces, cultures, and foods. I do not remember, however, specifically being taught that life is also a melting pot of experiences, the good the bad and the ugly. Beauty and despair.

I know we want experiences that are easy and euphoric and keep us in our cozy nest, but we are given instead, through abundant grace, distractions, failures, and frustrations. A quote from C.S. Lewis that is both my favorite and least favorite is this: "We are not necessarily doubting that God will do the best for us; we are wondering how painful the best will turn out to be."[43] It's a favorite because it is true. It's a least favorite because, well, it's true. We like the best for us, but we do not like pain.

James 1:2–4 tells us that we should be joyful in affliction, excited about the perseverance being produced as our faith is tested, because this makes us mature and complete, lacking nothing. He desires for us to lack nothing. In fact, Ephesians 1:3 says, "Praise be to the God and Father of our Lord Jesus Christ, who has blessed us in the heavenly realms with every spiritual blessing in Christ." (NIV) We have, in fact, been given everything through Christ, making Him our greatest need. But, because Christ is our greatest need, we cannot *lack nothing* until we have been stripped of everything that is not of Him. But like Wolterstorff's quote reads, as we look up in anguish, "We strain to hear, but instead of hearing an answer we catch sight of God himself scraped and torn. Through our tears we see the tears of God."[44]

Whether you are currently in the throes of a difficult time of life, sitting in a *one-of-those-days* days, years out from one where healing might still need to arrive, or in preparation for an inevitable time to come, take these words from Isaiah 7:4 with you: "Be careful, keep calm, and don't be afraid." (NIV) Do not lose heart.

Be careful. Do not purposely put yourself in places that you know are going to trigger bad thoughts and feelings before you are able to remember the moments without reliving them. However loved and protected we are, there is evil out there that definitely wants to destroy any chance we have of knowing, abiding in, and hoping in Christ. Look carefully how you walk, not as unwise but as wise (Ephesians 5:15); do not believe every spirit, test to see if it is God (1 John 4:1); walk by His Spirit. (Galatians 5:16)

Keep calm if those days happen, the ones with the potential to bring you crumbling down. I am the queen of flipping out and thinking later. The times I have had to apologize to my children, husband, God, friends, strangers, and myself for losing my composure before thinking things through is a number higher than even I want to attempt to count. But He gives us peace—not peace like the world, but perfect peace so that our hearts do not have to be troubled (John 14:27), and He promises that He will walk through the raging water and consuming fire with us. (Isaiah 43:2)

So, **do not fear**. The scale that we feel dipping constantly back and forth between beauty and despair is never really on the verge of toppling over. In truth, God, His Son, and His Spirit are fully present on both sides so that one never outweighs the other. In every beauty, there is an understanding of despair that would come if we did not have Him to call on, and in every despair there is an understanding of beauty because He is always with us.

Remember, hope always exists in every place hopelessness tries to overtake.

> *"Trust in the dark, trust in the light, trust at night and trust in the morning, and you will find that the faith that many begin, perhaps by a mighty effort, will end, sooner or later, by becoming the easy and natural habit of the soul."*[45]

The past longs to haunt you, to bring you back down to where you were or who you used to be, but all the while God is reminding you that you are not who you were; you are a new creation, being renewed day by day. Faith changes you, faith guides you to know hope. Hope is there no matter what change comes later. And that hope, even though it can't change what has happened in your past, has the potential to change what happens in another's future.

As you learn to cling to hope and as your faith, which starts with belief and grows into trust, then matures into confidence, you do not just become a follower of hope; you become a steward of it. And because of that, you can carry that same hope you found in the darkest of places to other people still in the dark.

Darkness is an inevitable part of our every day. It comes like clockwork, the light of the day ending, intended to give us the rest and refreshment of sleep and the ability to recoup before the light of the next day appears. But for some, there is also an uneasiness that occurs as the light disappears. Objects are no longer clearly seen, and unknowns monumentally outweigh the known that comes through clear sight bathed in light. Studies even suggest that the *witching hour* that all parents are way too familiar with is caused by the ingrained knowledge that the sun is setting and darkness is coming.

But God separated the light from the dark in the first part of Genesis and called them both *good*. Yes, darkness reminds our bodies to rest, but darkness also reminds us what it is like without light. Likewise, dark times remind us and others of how much we need the light of Christ in our lives. As a believer, as a steward of the hope you have been given, it is not enough to just know there is light in the darkness; we must also go into the darkness carrying the light we have been given.

I cannot be a light in the darkness if I am not willing to step into it.

Life will be full of God-given opportunities to open the doors to dark tunnels and step down into the depths while carrying with you the only light you need. The light is ignited by the hope you hold on to, the hope you found out of hopelessness, the hope that is forever clinging to you. There is not enough time or space to describe the infinite doors that can be opened to search in darkness. One only has to step a few feet into the world, into the life of another, to find an opportunity. Everyone has a story. Everyone has a hurt. They will all be different, but that same hope that carries you through is the same hope that will carry them as well.

Looking on the surface will grant you the ability to see beautiful things the way the world sees them, but you will miss the infinite amount of beauty that the world's eyes will never be able to see. Below the surface, in the darkness of where God's redeeming power shines light as He shoots one arrow after another into each and every hidden corner, we see the beauty of redeeming grace, of change brought through faith, and of faith that leads us to know true hope.

Today, this part of my past has no hold on me. Even when those days come, I no longer want to give up, because I know hope, I know the promise, I know that even if I slide back, hope holds on. I know that though the darkness was all around me, the darkness was not dark to Him, because He is with me and He is light, and that light shines hope like a beacon in the rubble.

There will come a day when the past no longer has a hold on you. When you will not crumble as quickly or as often, and you won't remember the last time that anything drove you to that posture. But there is no timeline for healing from any situation. You may run, you may walk, you may crawl, you may get stuck several times on the journey. The reason there is no timeline for healing is because time will not heal your wounds.

Though the saying *Time heals all wounds* has been around since Chaucer supposedly coined the phrase, it only takes a quick search to see that while it is flippantly and at times lovingly spoken as encouragement, it is a lie that not only does not help, but can cause further hurt.

Time is only a way we track how long a process is taking. It aids our finite minds in keeping a count of the comings and goings of minutes, hours, days, months, and years. Time, on its own, produces nothing. If we allow time to heal, what we are truly doing is sitting and waiting for a set of measurements to take away our pain. Believe me, I understand what the saying means, but I want to encourage you to look past a set of words and to remember what truly brings the lasting healing.

When our bodies are scratched, bruised, and broken, it does take time for them to heal, but time is not what is doing the healing. I have watched a cut on a finger bleed, scab over, and then disappear as if it were never there. Time did not heal that finger; the amazing properties God gave our skin to replenish itself healed that finger. If badly injured, you would not just wait for time to go by, hoping to get better. Your injury could become more severe, infection could set in, a small cold could progress into a life-threatening illness if left untreated. Waiting is good; waiting without assistance, however, can do damage.

Our hearts and spirits are the same.

When we are wounded emotionally and spiritually, time will not heal our pain. Rose Kennedy said, "It has been said time heals all wounds, I do not agree. The wounds remain. In time, the mind, protecting its sanity, covers them with scar tissue and the pain lessens, but it is never gone." I am inclined to agree with her. The mind will work that way, protecting itself, shoving things in boxes in the far corners, hiding hurts away, and if that is what continues, the wounds will never be gone; they will just stay hidden until something drags them back to the forefront, needing to be shoved once again into their perfectly labeled box.

True healing comes from hope, from clinging to the promises of the future.

There will be a day when the past you know now will no longer have a hold on you, but life does not stop. Once we make it through one difficult experience, chances are another will find its way into our lives. The beauty of hope is that, the next time, hopelessness will not grab hold of you as tightly when you remember the truths you have found, the truths that have found you. Wait for it with patience; wait for hope to float in and overpower the fear. Wait as light pierces the darkness, and then take that light further into the dark to shine it for others. Wait for the hope to remind you that the promises you are clinging to are always clinging to you.

9

Continuing to Cling

Wednesday night Mexican has been a tradition for years, just me and one of the greatest friends God can grant a person sitting opposite each other in a booth. Chicken quesadilla on one side and two carne asada tacos on the other with a bowl of cheese dip in between. The food does not change, but the hearts and words that are shared vary from week to week. Some weeks my ears are perked as she spills more about the life she is currently enduring; other weeks she listens as I go on and on between bites about the ups and downs of my current events. Sometimes it is a constant back and forth as we trade off words of frustration and words of encouragement, and then there are times we sit a little quieter, enjoying moments of peace.

The one-year anniversary of the dropping of the bomb that led to this journey of hope had arrived, and on that particular Wednesday night my friend's husband was out of town, which meant she couldn't meet up at our usual place. Take-out order in hand, I showed up at her home and we sat again, this time at her kitchen table, with a chicken quesadilla on one side and two carne asada tacos on the other, with cheese dip in between. We reminisced about the past year, about the glory of God and His faithfulness over everything. As we rejoiced in the fact that a year had passed, tears began to stream down my cheeks.

A year is such a long time, and yet, a year is also so very short. So many strides had been made, so many aspects were better, more beautiful. Yet my mind began to reel off everything that still needed improvement, everything that still brought pain. She reached over and grabbed my hand and, as if reading my mind, looked me in the eyes and said, "It's only been a year." Praise God for a year behind us, a year of the first anniversaries of dates I never wanted to circle on the calendar. But praise God, it's only been a year, and He's not finished yet.

British accents, a beautiful countryside, powerful music, an independent female character, and a soft but strong man who inevitably sweeps her off her feet. There seems to be a trend in the films that hold their place in my top ten. *Pride and Prejudice* is affectionately known as my crafting movie and always seems to be on when creative juices are flowing. *Sense and Sensibility* is the go-to every time I feel under the weather. Its mix of heartache and happy endings never fails to give me a boost. *About Time*, though not a period movie, has made me ponder how I desire to live my life more than any movie I have ever seen, and even *The Sound of Music*, my always number one, although set in Austria, has lead actors that never tried to hide the British lilt behind their voices.

Another I have recently added to the list did not have the royal overtones of *P&P* or the quick wit and fast speak of *S&S*, but *Far from the Madding Crowd*, based on Thomas Hardy's novel, contained all the consistent characteristics that immediately capture my heart and added in was a character so patient and steadfast that for days after I could not help but focus on that trait alone.

God uses the world around us to speak to our hearts. Through His Word, obviously, through the community around us, and very often, for me at least, through works of art. "The heavens declare the glory of God," says Psalm 19 (ESV) and if, since the creation of the world, God's invisible qualities—for example, His eternal power and divine nature—have been clearly seen and understood from what has been made so that people are without excuse (Romans 1:20), surely it is not an odd leap to see Him and hear Him through the venues inspired by creation itself.

Once a ponderer, always a ponderer, and what better way to get lost in thoughts than through a world that is not your own. However, I am more than a little amused that my version of escaping reality through cinema is very often God's version of getting me exactly where He wants me to be. Well played, Sir, well played.

The question is, where are you?

Have you just made it through? Have you just begun? Are you sitting squarely in the middle with no view of either end? Are you so close to the finish line you can taste it? Can you look over your shoulder, still seeing the starting point, and want to run back and stay in that known place because the fear of the changing unknown is too much? We all find ourselves some-where; or maybe it feels as if we are all lost somewhere. Either way, our travels are rarely easy.

As an adult, I read a children's adaptation of *Pilgrim's Progress* by John Bunyan entitled *Dangerous Journey*.[46] I had every inten-tion of reading the original version as well, but, number one, I am a lover of children's literature, and number two, the original is much harder to understand. Maybe in this circumstance, I am stretching Jesus's meaning of coming to Him like little children, but I am holding to it anyway! In any case, the famous allegory tells well the trials of the Christian journey, and as we sit in our own trials, steadfast and patient is not where we always long to be, and yet it is in that space of waiting, as God reveals His plan to us step by step, moment by moment, that we are placed.

We've talked about how time does not heal our wounds. But if we are being honest with ourselves, don't we wish that it would? Knowing the timeline for healing would give us our deadline for hurt. Each morning it would be lovely to walk into the kitchen and rip off a piece of paper on the daily count-down, revealing a number smaller by one until, as they dwindle before our eyes, we get to the day when suddenly everything will feel normal again. We want the tangible assurance; God instead gives us the promise that requires the faithful wait.

As much as we have come to understand about hope and its present protection and future promise, as much faithfulness as we have seen God exemplify in the past, the question of whether or not it will happen again seeps in when, in your limited view, you see stagnation instead of fruition. Efficiency, that desire to just be done already in the quickest and best way possible, is hard to see when staying still, so the temptation to take matters into your own hands in various ways comes over us. It is tempting, as you sit and wait to see what God is going to do, to run instead. Only this time you don't want to run away. You want to run forward. You want to bolt through each step, as if the floor beneath your feet were hot lava, and get to the finish line.

If you ask my boys, *running* is always the answer. *Why walk when you can run?* It will get you there faster, obviously, and isn't faster always better? Running, however, often results in tripping over an obstacle you did not see because of your full-out sprint, resulting in being sprawled out on the grass crying in pain over whatever was just injured, hypothetically speaking of course.

Okay, so maybe running isn't always a great idea. How about a shortcut? If you are stuck in one place, you may think it's because there is something blocking the way, so instead of waiting, you forge another path on your own, assuming that it will get you to the same destination. If you are blessed with the ingrained map skills of my husband, this is a tricky lesson to learn from, because you might truly end up at the correct location in the end; but how much panic, frustration, and confusion came along the way as you wove in and out of unmarked and darkened streets to get there? However, if you have an extreme lack of directional skills like myself, the lesson is easy to learn, as the short cut method just gets you stuck somewhere you were not planning to go, and the only way out is to backtrack or call for help.

So fine, don't run ahead and don't take short cuts. I have learned my lesson, so I'll just sit right here and wait and you can tell me to get up when we're there. Except, actually, as contrary as this sounds, just sitting there is not what we are being asked to do either. Especially since our human minds can turn waiting into sitting crisscross applesauce on the road to the next thing, twiddling our thumbs assuming that when the opportune time comes we can just stand back up again and go merrily about our way. I love what Oswald Chambers said: "[W]e are to rest in the Lord, not to rust."[47] I can't help but think of the Tin Man frozen on the side of the road. No, it takes a good bit of oil to get back on our feet after closing ourselves up. Active participation, the gift of being involved in this life our Creator purposely formed: that is our role.

In the grown-up version of *Pilgrim's Progress*, Bunyan writes,

> *"This hill, though high, I covet to ascend;*
> *The difficulty will not me offend.*
> *For I perceive the way to life lies here.*
> *Come, pluck up, heart; let's neither faint nor fear.*
> *Better, though difficult, the right way to go,*
> *Than wrong, though easy, where the end is woe."*[48]

The easy way, the *efficient way*, is a way of woe, a way that does not allow the sufferings between to bring us to hope at the end. But rest assured the right way to go, though unknown, is held firmly in place by a known God who crafted each step before the beginning of time, whether you know where your feet will set down or not. "Faith is the confidence in what we hope for and assurance for what we do not see," says Hebrews 11:1 (NIV), just before rattling off the Hall of Faith, the ancients who walked with God without His complete Word that we now have, showing us His faithfulness time and time again. He IS faithful.

Just thinking about Abraham is mind boggling and humbling. Sitting in comfort and wealth, He is told to get up and move everything and everyone to a new place, and he does it. Sight unseen, he packs up his not-so-little world and faithfully follows the voice of God. Years later, after this land he was called to becomes his home, after he is given a child in the most impossible of circumstances, there is another story. The story of him and Isaac on the top of the mountain. Abraham hears God ask him to sacrifice his son and faithfully Abraham prepares, and his faithfulness is rewarded with a ram caught in the bushes, a sacrificial lamb. A precursor to the Lamb who would sacrifice Himself for us.

Faith is not blind; never let anyone accuse you of that. Abraham, the father of the nations, did not follow blindly. He followed with full view, not a view of what would happen, but a view of the God who makes it all happen. In Abraham's mind there was just the memory of time and time again when God said something and then came through, said and then came through, promise after promise, His God provided. Whatever doubts may have been in his mind did not stop the fact that His God, in whatever way, would provide for him, would hold him up with His righteous right hand.

As we walk this walk with hope, as you look at your circumstances or the circumstances of another, the problem is not whether or not God is directing the path, or whether Christ made the way or whether the Spirit is next to us on the road. That is and always will be true. Christ's work is done and that promise has already been fulfilled. The problem is whether or not we are faithfully and patiently waiting as we step into what will come next and what will continue after. Are we being steadfast?

Let Him show you how He will carry it all to completion in your life as you wait and walk steadfastly with Him. But to do that, you must be content with where He has placed you.

The stages of grief are alive and well, and they are not just reserved for the hardest of situations. You does not have to input their symptoms or scenarios in the system before the stages of grief are then released into your heart. The smallest and biggest of circumstances will release these fluid feelings of denial to acceptance, with multiple stops in between.

My personal favorite (well, *favorite* might be the wrong word)

164

is anger. In the aftermath of my husband's confession, and in the months and years that have followed, the fuse that was once long and winding, never really getting to the end, got cut off to a nub. Consequences ensued.

If at this moment we were somehow miraculously blessed with a daughter, she would be given what could be interpreted as a most grandma-sounding name. *Matilda Ruth May* would not only hold all of our hearts, but in turn would be granted a first name after one of my most favorite book characters and a middle name matching that of a woman in the Bible that has encouraged me since the first reading, decades ago.

Ruth was a girl who married a man who had moved from his land in Israel into her own, Moab. After the death of her husband, her husband's brothers, and her husband's father, she was left alone with her mother-in-law and her sister-in-law, who also happened to be from the same country as she. Though tradition and law would have kept her bound to her husband's family, when the decision was made to move back to the family's original homeland, her mother-in-law gave her an out, told her to stay in the place she knew, with the people she knew. Her sister-in-law took the opportunity to leave. Ruth stayed. And thus began a story that resulted in another link in the line of Jesus.

The thing is, Ruth didn't know that that was going to happen. No angel appeared to her, as did to Mary centuries later, to tell her she was going to give birth to a Savior. Ruth did not have the benefit of reading and studying her story in a bound book, as we have. All Ruth had was a brief moment on a road to make a decision to run back or keep going. No one would have faulted her for either choice.

That moment when you step forward, when you keep

following in faith, when you remain steadfast in Him while resting in hope, brings you a peace, a relief, a joy that cannot be compared to anything else.

The phrase *glean in the field where you are planted* came from an in-depth study I did in college on the book of Ruth. Wherever you find yourself, take advantage of the opportunity, learn all you can from the experience so that that knowledge can become wisdom and prepare you for whatever is to come next. Remember, piece by piece He builds us up, lesson by lesson our sufferings transition us into the place of sitting in hope. But again, I have learned—the hard way, I might add—that to glean, like to remain steadfast, you must be content with where He has placed you.

Have you ever tried to be content with where you are while also being furious with where you are? Those two feelings do not mix. You cannot be content with where God has you if you are furious for being there. But believe me, BELIEVE ME, when I say it is OKAY if contentment is not an immediate reaction. For someone who is constantly carrying around that undesired side effect of a short fuse as a result from her past hurts, fury is definitely a stop on the trip to contentment. It is OKAY to get mad and frustrated, with an array of other emotional pit stops thrown in as well.

If fury or anything else besides contentment is what you are feeling now, let God know. Do not try to push past it or ignore it or fix it on your own. Your unrelentingly loving Father can handle all of you and longs to do so. He knows your heart and is forever refining you on the way, so tell Him what you're feeling.

There are words that can be substituted for *contentment. Pleasure, cheerfulness,* and *gratification* are just a few, but in this conversation of being content with where God has placed each of us, the only word I can think to use is *satisfied*. God longs for and asks us to let Him satisfy. The original four-line text that so calmed my heart included this very idea. *Be satisfied in Him alone.* Let Him fill up all the places inside us so that we are satisfied in Him and Him alone. To see satisfaction elsewhere is to place something else in His place, above where He should rest in our lives.

Using Psalm 90:14 as inspiration, our friend Mike Kinnebrew wrote a beautiful song in which he sings, "Satisfy us Lord, with your tender mercies, that we may rejoice, that we may be glad, all our days."

It can be difficult to understand this concept of contentment in the middle of a bomb-exploding, life-altering situation. I spent three decades of life with the completely wrong understanding of the word *contentment*. For me, *contentment* meant *to make do, to make the best of*. In friendships, in romantic relationships, in work experiences, there was this thought that no matter what happened, I just had to live with it, make the best of it, fix it so that it appeared better or so that I appeared okay, *content*. I put myself in control. And self-righteousness just reared its hideous head for thirty-two years, until God so lovingly entered time and space to expose its dangers.

I am with you when you say the hardest part is knowing whether to seek contentment and wait for change or to seek contentment and look for change or to conclude that contentment doesn't need to be found because a change of direction does. Are the rocks I am pushing uphill needed to build whatever is at the peak, or are they just getting in the way and need to be let go of so that my hands will be free for whatever I find to do at the top?

When these questions come up, it's time for me to listen to these words from Gerald Sittser instead of the doubts that come up: "No matter what our circumstances, we can enter right now into God's will for us—the will of a wise and loving Father who knows how to weave all of our choices into a redemptive masterpiece."[49] That is our hope. That is our future promise. Whether I keep pushing an unnecessary boulder or whether I let one go that might have been helpful to have after all, I can be content in whatever state I find myself in next, because He redeems it all; He *has* redeemed it all.

Like many other things, my previous lack of contentment often came from fear. I was afraid to be content because I was afraid God would make me stay where I was forever or forget that I wanted to move on to something else eventually. But He knows the desires of our hearts and asking Him for something is not a sign of discontentment, so long as I trust Him no matter what His answer is.

If you're seeking contentment for where you are in life so that you can walk faithfully with Him in hope through difficult trials, I share with you this conversation between singer/songwriters Andrew Osenga and Bebo Norman from Osenga's podcast, *The Pivot*.

It's okay to try something and for it to go well and for it to not go well. It's okay to walk away from something that is going really well because you are not meant to do it. You can be about pursuing something and come to the conclusion that it is not something you need to continue pursuing. You can be about pursuing something and know it's something you do not want to continue pursuing but have no choice at the moment to not do it because of the commitment you have made. Even the next thing you are sure you are supposed to do may not work and then you will find yourself back at square one again. The gift is knowing that whatever hurdle comes, it doesn't end who you are, your identity in Christ. Life does not fall apart just because of a shift in your current state.[50]

We are, at our core, unshakable when we rest in the hope of His promise. "Rest in God alone, oh my soul," the psalmist says. "For my hope comes from Him. He alone is my rock and my salvation; He is my fortress, I will not be shaken." (Psalm 62:5–6, NIV) Christ gives us freedom from caring about the end result by enabling us to be content in the midst of whatever. Nothing is wasted. But life in Christ is not passive. Yes, God is sovereign and holds the entirety of my story in His hands, completely crafted from eternity, but it takes my physical movement to go forward on this earth. We just cannot go it alone.

Clinging to hope is all well and good, but if it's by our own strength, we will give out. If it's by our own power, we will fail. If it's by our own mind, we will crumble. We were not built for independence, but we try to accomplish it anyway, coming up short. This determination to go it alone is one reason why we look at ourselves and are displeased, why we spend so much time trying to reach a goal that we never seem to be satisfied with. We always find fault with how well we're keeping up, how well we're performing, how well we're trying to prove that we can find hope and hold on alone. I know I do.

Ive never really liked my hands. My sister inherited the good hands. Hers are soft and smooth, long fingers with nails that grow past the point where the white actually shows and can be filed in a ladylike manner. I seem to have inherited the opposite. Even at a young age they seemed, to my eyes, like old lady hands. I got the large veins that show their blue through the skin on the back, short fingernails that break too easily, and no amount of lotion will keep them soft and supple for long.

You would think that the five years of CrossFit they have endured would make me like them less, because now added in with what was previously mentioned are calluses and torn blisters and the scars that are still slightly visible from previous ones that have already healed. But actually, that makes me like them a little more, because at least I can see with my eyes the work they have done. If I can't have pretty, at least I can have productive. But there is one aspect of those two extremities at the end of my arms that I just can't seem to improve, which is how well they can hold on.

It never fails, or I guess I should say *they always fail*. Sooner or later, usually sooner rather than later, they give out and let go. All the willpower in the world cannot make them hold a bar for longer than they are able. I have to stop and rest them, shake them out, and will them to try again. Recently, after having a seemingly normal conversation—well, normal for some of us—about grip strength and bar cycling with one of our coaches, I sat in the car staring at my battle wounds, and gained a sense of understanding. Yes, I can improve their strength; our bodies were created in an amazing way that makes growth and improvement a possibility. But I will never be able to hold on to anything forever. Why? Because I was not built to hold on. I was built to be held on to.

A story I was told years ago has always stayed with me. In the story, a man's friend was on a tubing trip with his family. As they floated peacefully down the river, his young daughter in his lap, the water's current started to quicken, and before them they saw that the rapids that were usually quiet had grown fierce and wild with the recent rain. He braced himself for the blows to come, and with all his might held tightly to his daughter as they were thrown from the tube and sent into the waters.

Tumbling and turning, he kept holding on to her until they finally reached calm waters again. With tears streaming down her face, she grinned proudly at her daddy and said, "I holded on, I holded on the whole time!" Yes, she did her best, she held on as hard as she was able; but he knew the truth. You see, she was not safe because of her strength to hold on, she was safe because someone stronger was holding on to her, and he never let go.

It is a lesson I have learned a thousand times for sure, with thousands left to go. I cannot control the outcome, I can only fulfill my part. I cannot force things to happen that are not meant to be, just like I cannot stop what is meant to be from happening. I can cling and stretch and learn and grow, all good things to be sure, but eventually I will have to let go, and when I do I can clearly see the One who is always holding on to me. In my weakness I see His strength, in my weakness He in me makes me strong.

As I continue and practice, strength will grow in these hands of mine, and maybe I will be able, bit by bit, to hold on a little longer. But as far as my spirit goes, maybe the lesson should be to let go a little sooner so that I can rest in my Father who never lets go.

It is in seeing hope hold on to us that gives us the capacity to carry hope with us into the next thing and the next thing and the next. We are being made new; for all the days we walk with Him, from the first breath of acceptance to the last breath we take, we are being made new. Newness of heart, this lifelong sanctification process, requires all the peaks and valleys, all the lines on the monitor that show us life is still there. Hopelessness will grab at you again. But just like a yo-yo on an escalator, even if you still go round and round with the same situations, you are always traveling higher and are better able to see. And I pray that in those moments, you will see that there is always hope.

~ EPILOGUE ~
So, Speak Up!

When asked a question or confronted with a topic, it takes a while for me to process an answer, to think of exactly what I want to say, especially in a group setting, which means that whatever the topic *is* usually turns into *had been* as the others involved keep rolling, immediately knowing the best thing to say and whizzing past me as I sit, still trying to formulate my sentences. Because of this, I spent years thinking that my words were not important, that I did not have anything productive to add to the conversation because I could not keep up long enough to add anything in!

While silence can be deafening, remaining silent can also make you feel deaf, make you feel out of the loop, make you feel inconsequential. When you spend your life assuming you have nothing to say, you forget how to speak up, even if you do have words that need to come out.

But words are not to be tread through lightly. Words harm and words heal. The phrase *If you don't have anything nice to say then don't say anything at all* is well-shared within the southern states.

It is also well-known that if you're told hundreds of wonderful, positive things about yourself, and then one negative, it is the negative that will stay with you the longest. It is for these reasons that we are told in Ephesians to be kind to one another and to let no unwholesome word come out of our mouths, but only what is good for building others up, so that it gives grace to those who hear it.

Our lives revolve around communication. Even in the most isolated places on earth there is language, the ability to speak and respond in some manner so that community can work together, rejoice together, disagree with one another, and warn each other of danger. Unless you are under the age of four, though, you cannot just go around saying aloud every thought that comes through your mind. Honestly, the under-four category probably shouldn't do that either, but so far I have yet to find someone with the skills to enable that filter.

Filters are valuable. They strain out impurities so that what you are taking in holds only that which is good for you. In the world, this may be referred to as your conscience. Good ol' Jiminy Cricket sang a very catchy tune about letting your conscience be your guide, listening to the inner voice telling you what is right and wrong.[51] In Christianity, we believe this is the Holy Spirit. The Helper that Jesus left with His children here on earth living inside us and guiding us is our filter. Through Him, knowledge of the Word filters our words, actions, and thoughts, sifting out impurities and changing them to be more like Christ. A point worth mentioning, however, is that whether we follow the Holy Spirit's leading or not, we are still loved and forgiven and never left alone.

I know no one who does not have regrets over something they said that they wish they could take back, but it is not the words that you have said that I want to talk to you about. It is the ones that you have not said, the ones that you are holding onto inside.

When Maya Angelou said, "There is no greater agony than bearing an untold story inside you,"[52] I believe that she was not just referring to someone who wants to be an author, but for all of us as we are each living out a story. I believe that each life is a story written by the greatest Author, meticulously planned and allowing experiences that will mold and shape us to become what He has designed us to be at story's end. But within this life of beauty and despair, of joy mixed with sorrow, with the refining and rebuilding that needs to be done, we often want to pull away when the process gets difficult.

While much concentration is needed to learn to filter our words and only let out what is helpful to others, we use an equal amount of concentration to hold our words inside because of what others may think, or what consequences may come.

I held my words in for too long. I let the fear of what could come and doubt of what might have been happening keep me from speaking up, keep me from letting out those questions and answers that I knew the Spirit was filling up my heart with.

I have no doubt that what happened in my marriage's past was not my fault, but I do know that had I spoken those words out loud long before, something could have changed sooner.

I would be willing to bet there is at least one thing that even right now you are keeping inside, afraid to say out loud, because of how it might come across, how it will sound, how it makes you sound, because it may be wrong or because of what another may think as soon as you finish the sentence.

Friend, if you are scared to say something, that is usually a good sign that you need to say it!

Words can eat at you if you leave them hidden, causing the agony Ms. Angelou so eloquently spoke of. But even worse is leaving those words in the darkness, away from the light, where they can be twisted so violently that you begin to believe the lies instead of the Truth.

I will forever be grateful for the friend who had the courage to live out Proverbs 31:8 and speak up for me when I refused to speak up for myself. There are many things that cause someone to remain silent. There are times when those people are given the courage to speak up, and there are times when God tells us to speak up for them because, for whatever reason, they cannot formulate the words.

I have developed a simple two-step process for speaking up. The first step is to find someone to say your words to; the second step is to say them out loud.

Lucky for you, there are two people with you all the time that you can speak to. One is yourself and the other is God. Yes, having a bosom friend or spouse who will listen and love you no matter what you say is a pearl above price, but please do not think you need to drive anywhere, wait for your next girls' night/Bible study/community group/workout/counseling session or other event during which you might have conversation. The first priority is not to have your words heard. It is to give them a voice.

Next, say them out loud. Quite often this one small but not-so-small action is the only thing needed to bring healing and relief to your soul. It takes courage to speak aloud the things you have hidden, and as soon as the words have left your lips, there can be peace and understanding that what you have feared so much to say may not be scary after all. This one action is an act of faith, and that act is rewarded with a precious peace that passes all understanding.

Not everything we say out loud that has been bottled up will be right. We have hearts full of sin and our thoughts will be skewed; our opinions will be unjustified; our words will be full of envy, or unforgiveness, or doubt. Even if more steps need to be taken to process through whatever the words reveal, they will be out, confessed, given a voice, and brought into the light. THAT is when healing can begin, when perspective is given, when wisdom is gained, and when our inner dispositions begin to change.

You may say hard things, and you may hear harder things, but as 1 John 1:9 says, "He is faithful and just. He will cleanse us from all unrighteousness." (ESV)

I pray that you will give all the parts of your story a voice so He can do just that. I ask you pray the same for me.

Acknowledgments

Zach, your humility and willingness to have our story known is a show of love and support that fills my heart to overflowing. I pray our lives will bring love and healing to others.

To Dave Crandall, we would not be where we are today without your wisdom, guidance, friendship, and patience. Thank you for preaching about hope, teaching about hope, and sharing Hope to everyone around you.

To Leslie, you are the secure to my insecure, the stable to my emotional, the take it as it is to my but I want it my way, the chicken quesadilla to my steak taco. You are the best a girl can have, and I love that you are always by my side.

To Lisa, Morgan, Rebekah, Stephanie Housworth, Dara Lynn, Grace, Kiley, Michelle, Kayla, Krista, Bailey, and Magda, thank you for being on my team during the hardest moments, thank you for bearing my burdens, thank you for being the community God created us to be for one another.

To Megan, Jess V., Courtney, Natalie, Kirsten, April, Sally, and so many more for being there in moments even when you had no idea what you were being there for or for coming years after and showing and sharing friendship when my trust in others was broken.

To Dave, Ryan, Diane, Other Zach, and Katie for reading my very early copy and kindly giving your feedback, corrections, suggestions, and encouragement. I am beyond grateful that you sacrificed your time, wisdom, and talent for this project.

To Angela, for having a conversation with Daniel and thinking of me which has led to the much easier process of making this book a real life thing. Just that simple act made me feel known, loved, and way less stressed!

To Christina, for sharing your talents by producing the beautiful artwork for the cover. I love the ways God continues to show how he places people in your life in the past for continued meaning in the future.

To our families who continually love well, forgive well, listen well, and challenge well. May we all continue to grow in grace well into the future.

To those who have read my writing from early on and shared it with others. Chances are I will never be famous, but if even one can find Hope in the person of Christ through anything written or shared in love it will be an honor, a privilege, and a blessing.

To our Creator, thank you for your redeeming grace, our Savior for being the one and only Hope we have, and His Spirit left with us for guiding our hearts to find more of Him.

Verses of Hope

All verses ESV

Ezra 10:2
And Shecaniah the son of Jehiel, of the sons of Elam, addressed Ezra: "We have broken faith with our God and have married foreign women from the peoples of the land, but even now there is hope for Israel in spite of this."

Psalm 9:18
For the needy shall not always be forgotten,
and the hope of the poor shall not perish forever.

Psalm 33:18
Behold, the eye of the Lord is on those who fear him,
on those who hope in his steadfast love . . .

Psalm 33:22
Let your steadfast love, O Lord, be upon us,
even as we hope in you.

Psalm 39:7
"And now, O Lord, for what do I wait?
My hope is in you."

Psalm 42:5
Why are you cast down, O my soul,
and why are you in turmoil within me?
Hope in God; for I shall again praise him,
my salvation . . .

Psalm 62:10
Put no trust in extortion;
set no vain hopes on robbery;
if riches increase, set not your heart on them.

Psalm 65:5
By awesome deeds you answer us with righteousness,
O God of our salvation,
the hope of all the ends of the earth
and of the farthest seas . . .

Psalm 119:43
And take not the word of truth utterly out of my mouth,
for my hope is in your rules.

Psalm 119:49
Remember your word to your servant,
in which you have made me hope.

Psalm 119:74
Those who fear you shall see me and rejoice,

because I have hoped in your word.

Psalm 119:114
You are my hiding place and my shield;
I hope in your word.

Psalm 147:11
. . . but the Lord takes pleasure in those who fear him,
in those who hope in his steadfast love.

Proverbs 13:12
Hope deferred makes the heart sick,
but a desire fulfilled is a tree of life.

Proverbs 23:18
Surely there is a future,
and your hope will not be cut off.

Proverbs 26:12
Do you see a man who is wise in his own eyes?
There is more hope for a fool than for him.

Jeremiah 14:22
Are there any among the false gods of the nations that can bring
rain?
Or can the heavens give showers?
Are you not he, O Lord our God?
We set our hope on you,
for you do all these things.

Jeremiah 17:13
O Lord, the hope of Israel,
all who forsake you shall be put to shame;
those who turn away from you[a] shall be written in the earth,
for they have forsaken the Lord, the fountain of living water.

Jeremiah 23:16
Thus says the Lord of hosts: "Do not listen to the words of the prophets who prophesy to you, filling you with vain hopes. They speak visions of their own minds, not from the mouth of the Lord.

Jeremiah 29:11
For I know the plans I have for you, declares the Lord, plans for welfare and not for evil, to give you a future and a hope.

Jeremiah 31:17
There is hope for your future,
declares the Lord,
and your children shall come back to their own country.

Lamentations 3:21–29
But this I call to mind,
and therefore I have hope;
The steadfast love of the Lord never ceases;
his mercies never come to an end;
they are new every morning;
great is your faithfulness.
"The Lord is my portion," says my soul,
"therefore I will hope in him."
The Lord is good to those who wait for him,
to the soul who seeks him.

It is good that one should wait quietly
for the salvation of the Lord.
It is good for a man that he bear
the yoke in his youth.
Let him sit alone in silence
when it is laid on him;
let him put his mouth in the dust—
there may yet be hope . . .

Hosea 2:15
And there I will give her her vineyards
and make the Valley of Achor a door of hope.
And there she shall answer as in the days of her youth,
as at the time when she came out of the land of Egypt.

Jonah 2:8
Those who pay regard to vain idols
forsake their hope of steadfast love.

Matthew 12:21
". . . and in his name the Gentiles will hope."

Acts 2:26
. . . therefore my heart was glad, and my tongue rejoiced;
my flesh also will dwell in hope.

Romans 4:18
In hope he believed against hope, that he should become the father
of many nations, as he had been told, "So shall your offspring be."

Romans 5:1–5

Therefore, since we have been justified by faith, we have peace with God through our Lord Jesus Christ. Through him we have also obtained access by faith[b] into this grace in which we stand, and we rejoice in hope of the glory of God. Not only that, but we rejoice in our sufferings, knowing that suffering produces endurance, and endurance produces character, and character produces hope, and hope does not put us to shame, because God's love has been poured into our hearts through the Holy Spirit who has been given to us.

Romans 8:20–25

For the creation was subjected to futility, not willingly, but because of him who subjected it, in hope that the creation itself will be set free from its bondage to corruption and obtain the freedom of the glory of the children of God. For we know that the whole creation has been groaning together in the pains of childbirth until now. And not only the creation, but we ourselves, who have the firstfruits of the Spirit, groan inwardly as we wait eagerly for adoption as sons, the redemption of our bodies. For in this hope we were saved. Now hope that is seen is not hope. For who hopes for what he sees? But if we hope for what we do not see, we wait for it with patience.

Romans 12:12

Rejoice in hope, be patient in tribulation, be constant in prayer.

Romans 15:4

For whatever was written in former days was written for our instruction, that through endurance and through the encouragement of the Scriptures we might have hope.

Romans 15:12
And again Isaiah says,
"The root of Jesse will come,
even he who arises to rule the Gentiles;
in him will the Gentiles hope."

Romans 15:13
May the God of hope fill you with all joy and peace in believing,
so that by the power of the Holy Spirit you may abound in hope.

1 Corinthians 9:10
Does he not certainly speak for our sake? It was written for our sake, because the plowman should plow in hope and the thresher thresh in hope of sharing in the crop.

1 Corinthians 13:13
So now faith, hope, and love abide, these three; but the greatest of these is love.

1 Corinthians 15:19
If in Christ we have hope in this life only, we are of all people most to be pitied

2 Corinthians 1:7
Our hope for you is unshaken, for we know that as you share in our sufferings, you will also share in our comfort.

2 Corinthians 1:10
He delivered us from such a deadly peril, and he will deliver us. On him we have set our hope that he will deliver us again.

2 Corinthians 3:12
Since we have such a hope, we are very bold . . .

Galatians 5:5
For through the Spirit, by faith, we ourselves eagerly wait for the hope of righteousness.

Ephesians 1:12
. . . so that we who were the first to hope in Christ might be to the praise of his glory.

Ephesians 1:18
. . . having the eyes of your hearts enlightened, that you may know what is the hope to which he has called you, what are the riches of his glorious inheritance in the saints,

Ephesians 2:12
. . . remember that you were at that time separated from Christ, alienated from the commonwealth of Israel and strangers to the covenants of promise, having no hope and without God in the world.

Ephesians 2:13
But now in Christ Jesus you who once were far off have been brought near by the blood of Christ.

Colossians 1:5
. . . because of the hope laid up for you in heaven. Of this you have heard before in the word of the truth, the gospel . . .

Colossians 1:23
. . . if indeed you continue in the faith, stable and steadfast, not

shifting from the hope of the gospel that you heard, which has been proclaimed in all creation under heaven, and of which I, Paul, became a minister.

Colossians 1:27
To them God chose to make known how great among the Gentiles are the riches of the glory of this mystery, which is Christ in you, the hope of glory.

1 Thessalonians 1:3
. . . remembering before our God and Father your work of faith and labor of love and steadfastness of hope in our Lord Jesus Christ.

1 Thessalonians 2:19
For what is our hope or joy or crown of boasting before our Lord Jesus at his coming? Is it not you?

1 Thessalonians 4:13
But we do not want you to be uninformed, brothers, about those who are asleep, that you may not grieve as others do who have no hope.

1 Thessalonians 5:8
But since we belong to the day, let us be sober, having put on the breastplate of faith and love, and for a helmet the hope of salvation.

1 Timothy 5:5
She who is truly a widow, left all alone, has set her hope on God and continues in supplications and prayers night and day . . .

1 Timothy 6:17
As for the rich in this present age, charge them not to be haughty,

nor to set their hopes on the uncertainty of riches, but on God, who richly provides us with everything to enjoy.

Titus 2:13
. . . waiting for our blessed hope, the appearing of the glory of our great God and Savior Jesus Christ . . .

Hebrews 10:23
Let us hold fast the confession of our hope without wavering, for he who promised is faithful.

1 Peter 1:3
Blessed be the God and Father of our Lord Jesus Christ! According to his great mercy, he has caused us to be born again to a living hope through the resurrection of Jesus Christ from the dead . . .

1 Peter 1:13
Therefore, preparing your minds for action, and being sober-minded, set your hope fully on the grace that will be brought to you at the revelation of Jesus Christ.

1 Peter 1:13
. . . who through him are believers in God, who raised him from the dead and gave him glory, so that your faith and hope are in God.

1 Peter 3:15
. . . but in your hearts honor Christ the Lord as holy, always being prepared to make a defense to anyone who asks you for a reason for the hope that is in you; yet do it with gentleness and respect . . .

1 John 3:3

And everyone who thus hopes in him purifies himself as he is pure.

Sources

1   C.S. Lewis, *The Four Loves*, 1960.

2   Allers, Roger, Rob Minkoff, Don Hahn, Irene Mecchi, Jonathan Roberts, Linda Woolverton, Jonathan Taylor Thomas, *The Lion King*, 2003.

3   Susan Conroy, *Mother Teresa's Lessons of Love and Secrets of Sanctity. Our Sunday Visitor*, 2003.

4   Kristen Welch, "And So We Weep," *We Are That Family*, February 23, 2016, wearethatfamily.com/2016/and-so-we-weep/.

5   *Hamilton: An American Musical*. Performances by Lin-Manuel Miranda, Leslie Odom Jr., Phillipa Soo, and Jonathan Groff. Atlantic Records, 2015.

6   Frederick Buechner, *Beyond Words: Daily Readings in the ABC's of Faith*. San Francisco, CA. HarberOne, May 11, 2004.

7   "The Most Dangerous World Ever?," Policy Report, CATO Institute, updated September/October 2014, https://www.cato.org/policy-report/septemberoctober-2014/most-dangerous-world-ever.

8   Marshall, Catherine, *A Closer Walk*. Edited by Leonard E. Sourd. Old Tappan, New Jersey: Fleming H. Revell Compa-

ny, 1986.

9   Tina Moore and Natalie Musumeci, "Young Manhattan dietitian Tara Condell hanged herself after posting suicide note," Metro, *New York Post*, updated January 31, 2019, https://nypost.com/2019/01/31/young-manhattan-nutritionist-hanged-herself-after-posting-suicide-note/.

10   John Lasseter, Andrew Stanton, Joe Ranft, Donald McEnery, Bob Shaw, Dave Foley, Kevin Spacey, Julia Louis-Dreyfus, Hayden Panettiere, Phyllis Diller, Richard Kind, David H. Pierce, and Randy Newman. *A Bug's Life*, 2000.

11   *Dictionary.com*, "Shame," accessed July 25, 2019, https://www.dictionary.com/browse/shame?s=t

12   Brene Brown, *I Thought It Was Just Me: Women Reclaiming Power and Courage in a Culture of Shame.* New York: Gotham, 2007.

13   Jill Phillips, "Nobody's Got it All Together," track 1 on *Nobody's Got It All Together*, Square Peg Alliance, 2006, compact disc.

14   N.T. Wright, *Early Christian Letters for Everyone: James, Peter, John, and Judah.* Westminster John Knox Press, 2015.

15   Scott J. Hafemann, *The God of Promise and the Life of Faith: Understanding the Heart of the Bible.* Crossway Books, 2001.

16   Paul D. Tripp, *New Morning Mercies: A Daily Devotion.* Crossway Books, 2016.

17   "The Truth Project: Do You Really Believe That What You Believe Is Really Real?", General, The Family Foundation, updated February 22, 2010. http://www.familyfoundation.org/blog-posts/2010/02/the-truth-project-do-you-really-believe-that-what-you-believe-is-really-real.

18   Andrew Peterson, *The Wingfeather Saga.* Nashville: Rabbit Room Press, 2008–2015.

19   Google Dictionary, s.v. "abide," accessed October 17,

2014, https://googledictionary.freecollocation.com/meaning?word=abide.

20 Google Dictionary, s.v. "abide," accessed October 17, 2014, https://googledictionary.freecollocation.com/meaning?word=abide.

21 Sally Lloyd-Jones and Jago, *The Jesus Storybook Bible: Every Story Whispers His Name.* Grand Rapids, Mich.: Enfield: Zondervan, 2007.

22 Romans 12:3, ESV.

23 John Piper, "Got has allotted to each a measure of faith," *Desiring God,* September 23, 1998, https://www.desiringgod.org/articles/god-has-allotted-to-each-a-measure-of-faith

24 Madeline L'Engle, *A Circle of Quiet: The Crosswicks Journal Book One.* HarperCollins Publishers, 1984.

25 Lara Williams. "Today's choices influence tomorrow's reality." *To Overflowing,* October 19, 2015, https://tooverflowing.com/todays-choices-influence-tomorrows-reality-remembering/.

26 Paul David Tripp, *New Morning Mercies: A Daily Gospel Devotional.* Wheaton, Illinois: Crossway, 2014.

27 Eric Metaxes, *Seven Women: And the Secret of Their Greatness.* Nashville, Tennessee: Nelson Books, 2015.

28 Sally Lloyd-Jones, *The Jesus Storybook Bible.* Grand Rapids, Michigan, Zonderkidz, 2007.

29 Manning, Brennan, *Abba's Child: The Cry of the Heart for Intimate Belonging.* Colorado Springs, Colorado: NavPress Publishing, 2002.

30 Wendell Berry, *Jayber Crow: A Novel.* Washington, D.C.: Counterpoint, 2000.

31 Nora Ephron, George Fenton, Nick Meyers, and Jeff Atmajian. *You've Got Mail.* USA, 1998.

32 Ray Blackston, Andrew Peterson, and cloudLibrary. *Flabbergasted*. [S.l.]: Oasis Audio, 2003.

33 Tripp, *New Morning Mercies: A Daily Devotion*.

34 R.J. Palacio, *Wonder*. London: Doubleday, 2012.

35 Malcolm Gladwell, *Outliers: The Story of Success*. New York: Little, Brown and Co., 2008

36 Dietrich Bonhoeffer, *Life Together*. London: SCM Press, 1954.

37 Bonhoeffer, *Life Together*.

38 Bonhoeffer, *Life Together*.

39 Wendell Berry, *Jayber Crow: A Novel*. Washington, D.C: Counterpoint, 2000.

40 Nicholas Wolterstorff, *Lament for a Son*. Grand Rapids, Michigan: Eerdmans, 1987.

41 L.M. Montgomery, *Anne of Green Gables*. New York: Bantam Books, 1976.

42 Judith Viorst and Ray Cruz, *Alexander and the Terrible, Horrible, No Good, Very Bad Day*. New York: Atheneum, 1977.

43 C.S. Lewis, *Letters to an American Lady*. Grand Rapids, Michigan: Wm. B. Eerdsmans Publishing Co., Reissue Edition, 2014.

44 Nicholas Wolterstorff, *Lament for a Son*. Grand Rapids, Mich.: Eerdmans, 1987.

45 Hannah Whitall Smith, *The Christian's Secret of a Happy Life*. Merchant Books. 2013.

46 Oliver Hunkin, *Dangerous Journey: The Story of* Pilgrim's Progress. Eerkmans Books for Young Readers, 1985.

47 Oswald Chambers, *The Golden Book of Oswald Chambers: My Utmost for His Highest; Selections for the Year*. New York: Dodd, Mead & Company, 1935.

48 John Bunyan, *The Pilgrim's Progress : from This World to That Which Is to Come*. Philadelphia; Chicago: S.I. Bell, 1891.

49 Gerald Lawson Sittser, *The Will of God as a Way of Life: Finding and Following the Will of Go*d. Zondervan Pub. House, 2000.

50 Andrew Osenga, "Bebo Norman," August 14, 2017, in *The Pivot: Stories of people who've made a change*, www.everybodypivots.com.

51 Walt Disney, Ben Sharpsteen, Hamilton S. Luske, Mel Blanc, Don Brodie, Walter Catlett, Marion Darlington, Frankie Darro, Cliff Edwards, Dickie Jones, Charles Judels, Jack Mercer, Patricia Page, Christian Rub, Evelyn Venable, Fred Moore, Frank Thomas, Milt Kahl, Vladimir Tytla, Ward Kimball, Art Babbitt, Eric Larson, Wolfgang Reitherman, Ted Sears, Otto Englander, Webb Smith, William Cottrell, Joseph Sabo, Erdman Penner, Aurelius Battaglia, Leigh Harline, Ned Washington, Paul J. Smith, and Carlo Collodi. *Pinocchio*. Burbank, CA: Walt Disney Studios Home Entertainment, 2009.

52 Harold Bloom, editor. Maya Angelou's *I Know Why the Caged Bird Sings*. New York :Chelsea House Publishers, 1996.

CPSIA information can be obtained
at www.ICGtesting.com
Printed in the USA
LVHW110752031120
670551LV00006B/373

9 781953 259028